Also by Ted Hughes

Poetry

THE HAWK IN THE RAIN

LUPERCAL

WODWO

CROW

GAUDETE

FLOWERS AND INSECTS

MOORTOWN

MOORTOWN DIARY

WOLFWATCHING

RAIN-CHARM FOR THE DUCHY

THREE BOOKS: *Remains of Elmet, Cave Birds, River*

ELMET *(with photographs by Fay Godwin)*

NEW SELECTED POEMS 1957–1994

BIRTHDAY LETTERS

Translations

SENECA'S OEDIPUS

WEDEKIND'S SPRING AWAKENING

LORCA'S BLOOD WEDDING

PHEDRE *(by Racine)*

THE ORESTEIA OF AESCHYLUS

Selections

SELECTED POEMS OF EMILY DICKENSON

SELECTED VERSE OF SHAKESPEARE

A CHOICE OF COLERIDGE'S VERSE

THE RATTLE BAG *(edited with Seamus Heaney)*

THE SCHOOL BAG *(edited with Seamus Heaney)*

TALES

FROM

OVID

TALES

FROM

OVID

TED

HUGHES

FARRAR STRAUS GIROUX

NEW YORK

Farrar, Straus and Giroux
18 West 18th Street, New York 10011

Copyright © 1997 by Ted Hughes
Distributed in Canada by Douglas & McIntyre Ltd.
Printed in the United States of America
Originally published in 1997 by Faber and Faber Ltd., Great Britain
Published in 1997 in the United States by Farrar, Straus and Giroux
First paperback edition, 1999

The Library of Congress has cataloged the hardcover edition as follows:
Ovid, 43 B.C.–17 or 18 A.D.

    [Metamorphoses. English. Selections]

    Tales from Ovid / [translated by] Ted Hughes.— 1st American ed.

      p. cm.

    Originally published: London, Faber & Faber, 1997.

    Comprises 24 stories from Metamorphoses.

    Includes bibliographical references.

    ISBN 0-374-22841-8 (alk. paper)

    1. Metamorphoses—Mythology—Poetry. 2. Mythology, Classical—
Poetry. I. Hughes, Ted, 1930– . II. Title.
PA6522.M2H78 1997
873'.01—dc21

97-36061

Paperback ISBN-13: 978-0-374-52587-3
Paperback ISBN-10: 0-374-52587-0

www.fsgbooks.com

19

CONTENTS

Introduction

Ovid was born the year after the death of Julius Caesar and flourished in the Rome of Augustus. He completed the *Metamorphoses* around the time of the birth of Christ, was later banished for some unknown offence against the Emperor, and spent the last ten years of his life in exile at Tomis on the Black Sea.

In its length and metre, the *Metamorphoses* resembles an epic. But the opening lines describe the very different kind of poem that Ovid set out to write: an account of how from the beginning of the world right down to his own time bodies had been magically changed, by the power of the gods, into other bodies.

This licensed him to take a wide sweep through the teeming underworld or overworld of Romanised Greek myth and legend. The right man had met the right material at the right moment. The *Metamorphoses* was a success in its own day. During the Middle Ages throughout the Christian West it became the most popular work from the classical era, a source-book of imagery and situations for artists, poets and the life of high culture. It entered English poetry at a fountainhead, as one of Chaucer's favourite books, which he plundered openly, sometimes—as with the tale of Pyramus and Thisbe—in quite close translation. A little later, it played an even more dynamic role for Shakespeare's generation—and perhaps for Shakespeare in particular. The "sweet, witty soul" of Ovid was said to live again in him. But perhaps

Shakespeare's closest affinity did not lie so much in the sweet, witty Ovidian facility for "smelling out the odoriferous flowers of fancy," as one of his characters put it, nor in his aptitude for lifting images or even whole passages nearly verbatim, nor in drawing from two stories in the *Metamorphoses* his own best-seller, the seminal long poem *Venus and Adonis*. A more crucial connection, maybe, can be found in their common taste for a tortured subjectivity and catastrophic extremes of passion that border on the grotesque. In this vein, Shakespeare's most Ovidian work was his first—*Titus Andronicus*. Thirty or so dramas later, in *Cymbeline*, his mild and blameless heroine Imogen—whom her beloved husband will try to murder, whom her loathed stepbrother will try to rape—chooses for her bedtime reading Ovid's shocking tale of Tereus and Philomela.

Different aspects of the poem continued to fascinate Western culture, saturating literature and art. And by now, many of the stories seem inseparable from our unconscious imaginative life.

Why the world should have so clasped Ovid's versions of these myths and tales to its bosom is a mystery. As a guide to the historic, original forms of the myths, Ovid is of little use. His attitude to his material is like that of the many later poets who have adapted what he presents. He, too, is an adaptor. He takes up only those tales which catch his fancy, and engages with each one no further than it liberates his own creative zest. Of those he does take up—about two hundred and fifty in all—he gives his full attention to only a proportion, sketching the others more briefly in ornamental digressions or cramming them as clusters of foreshortened portraits into some eddy of his unfurling drift.

Myths and fantastic legends, wonder-tales about the embroilment of the natural human world with the supernatural, obviously held a quite special attraction for him—as they have done for most people throughout history. But this aspect of his material, though it is usually dominant, does not altogether explain his addictive appeal for generations of imaginative artists. Nor does his urbane, cavalier lightness of touch, or the swiftness and filmic economy of his narrative, or the playful philosophical breadth of his detachment, his readiness to entertain every possibility, his strange yoking of incompatible moods. All these qualities are there, with many more, and all are important. But perhaps what has gone deepest into his long succession of readers, and brought him so intimately into the life of art, is what he shared with Shakespeare. Above all, Ovid was interested in passion. Or rather, in what a passion feels like to the one possessed by it. Not just ordinary passion either, but human passion *in extremis*—passion where it combusts, or levitates, or mutates into an experience of the supernatural.

This is the current he divines and follows in each of his tales—the current of human passion. He adapts each myth to this theme. Where details or complexities of the traditional story encumber or diffuse his theme, he simply omits them. He must have known the full myth of Venus and Adonis, in which the Goddess of Love and her opposite in the underworld, the Goddess of Death, quarrel for possession of the baby Adonis, and in which the Boar has multiple identities, and where the whole sequence of events completes the annual cycle of the sacrificed god. But all Ovid wants is the story of hopelessly besotted and doomed love in the most intense form imaginable—as suffered by the love-goddess herself.

The act of metamorphosis, which at some point touches each of the tales, operates as the symbolic guarantee that the passion has become mythic, has achieved the unendurable intensity that lifts the whole episode onto the supernatural or divine plane. Sometimes this happens because mortals tangle with gods, sometimes because mortal passion makes the breakthrough by sheer excess, without divine intervention—as in the tale of Tereus and Philomela. But in every case, to a greater or lesser degree, Ovid locates and captures the peculiar frisson of that event, where the all-too-human victim stumbles out into the mythic arena and is transformed.

However impossible these intensities might seem to be on one level, on another, apparently more significant level Ovid renders them with compelling psychological truth and force. In his earlier books, preoccupied with erotic love, he had been a sophisticated entertainer. Perhaps here, too, in the *Metamorphoses* he set out simply to entertain. But something else joined in, something emerging from the very nature of his materials yet belonging to that unique moment in history—the moment of the birth of Christ within the Roman Empire. The Greek/Roman pantheon had fallen in on men's heads. The obsolete paraphernalia of the old official religion were lying in heaps, like old masks in the lumber room of a theatre, and new ones had not yet arrived. The mythic plane, so to speak, had been defrocked. At the same time, perhaps one could say as a result, the Empire was flooded with ecstatic cults. For all its Augustan stability, it was at sea in hysteria and despair, at one extreme wallowing in the bottomless appetites and sufferings of the gladiatorial arena, and at the other searching higher and higher for a spiritual transcendence—which eventually did take form, on the crucifix. The tension between these extremes, and occasionally their collision, can be felt in these tales. They establish a rough register of what it feels like to live in the psychological gulf that opens at the end of an era. Among everything else that we see in them, we certainly recognise this.

TALES
FROM
OVID

Creation; Four Ages;
Lycaon; Flood

Now I am ready to tell how bodies are changed
Into different bodies.

I summon the supernatural beings
Who first contrived
The transmogrifications
In the stuff of life.
You did it for your own amusement.
Descend again, be pleased to reanimate
This revival of those marvels.
Reveal, now, exactly
How they were performed
From the beginning
Up to this moment.

Before sea or land, before even sky
Which contains all,
Nature wore only one mask—
Since called Chaos.
A huge agglomeration of upset.
A bolus of everything—but
As if aborted.
And the total arsenal of entropy
Already at war within it.

No sun showed one thing to another,
No moon

Played her phases in heaven,
No earth
Spun in empty air on her own magnet,
No ocean
Basked or roamed on the long beaches.

Land, sea, air, were all there
But not to be trodden, or swum in.
Air was simply darkness.
Everything fluid or vapour, form formless.
Each thing hostile
To every other thing: at every point
Hot fought cold, moist dry, soft hard, and the
    weightless
Resisted weight.

God, or some such artist as resourceful,
Began to sort it out.
Land here, sky there,
And sea there.
Up there, the heavenly stratosphere.
Down here, the cloudy, the windy.
He gave to each its place,
Independent, gazing about freshly.
Also resonating—
Each one a harmonic of the others,
Just like the strings
That would resound, one day, in the dome of the
    tortoise.

The fiery aspiration that makes heaven
Took it to the top.
The air, happy to be idle,
Lay between that and the earth
Which rested at the bottom

Engorged with heavy metals,
Embraced by delicate waters.

When the ingenious one
Had gained control of the mass
And decided the cosmic divisions
He rolled earth into a ball.
Then he commanded the water to spread out flat,
To lift itself into waves
According to the whim of the wind,
And to hurl itself at the land's edges.
He conjured springs to rise and be manifest,
Deep and gloomy ponds,
Flashing delicious lakes.
He educated
Headstrong electrifying rivers
To observe their banks—and to pour
Part of their delight into earth's dark
And to donate the remainder to ocean
Swelling the uproar on shores.

Then he instructed the plains
How to roll sweetly to the horizon.
He directed the valleys
To go deep.
And the mountains to rear up
Humping their backs.

Everywhere he taught
The tree its leaf.

Having made a pattern in heaven—
Two zones to the left, two to the right
And a fifth zone, fierier, between—
So did the Wisdom

Divide the earth's orb with the same:
A middle zone uninhabitable
Under the fire,
The outermost two zones beneath deep snow,
And between them, two temperate zones
Alternating cold and heat.

Air hung over the earth
By just so much heavier than fire
As water is lighter than earth.
There the Creator deployed cloud,
Thunder to awe the hearts of men,
And winds
To polish the bolt and the lightning.

Yet he forbade the winds
To use the air as they pleased.
Even now, as they are, within their wards,
These madhouse brothers, fighting each other,
All but shake the globe to pieces.

The East is given to Eurus—
Arabia, Persia, all that the morning star
Sees from the Himalayas.
Zephyr lives in the sunset.
Far to the North, beyond Scythia,
Beneath the Great Bear, Boreas
Bristles and turns.
Opposite, in the South,
Auster's home
Is hidden in dripping fog.
Over them all
Weightless, liquid, ether floats, pure,
Purged of every earthly taint.

Hardly had he, the wise one, ordered all this
Than the stars
Clogged before in the dark huddle of Chaos
Alit glittering in their positions.

And now to bring quick life
Into every corner
He gave the bright ground of heaven
To the gods, the stars and the planets.
To the fish he gave the waters.
To beasts the earth, to birds the air.

Nothing was any closer to the gods
Than these humble beings,
None with ampler mind,
None with a will masterful and able
To rule all the others.

Till man came.
Either the Maker
Conceiving a holier revision
Of what he had already created
Sculpted man from his own ectoplasm,
Or earth
Being such a new precipitate
Of the etheric heaven
Cradled in its dust unearthly crystals.

Then Prometheus
Gathered that fiery dust and slaked it
With the pure spring water,
And rolled it under his hands,
Pounded it, thumbed it, moulded it
Into a body shaped like that of a god.

Though all the beasts
Hang their heads from horizontal backbones
And study the earth
Beneath their feet, Prometheus
Upended man into the vertical—
So to comprehend balance.
Then tipped up his chin
So to widen his outlook on heaven.

In this way the heap of all disorder
Earth
Was altered.
It was adorned with the godlike novelty
Of man.

And the first age was Gold.
Without laws, without law's enforcers,
This age understood and obeyed
What had created it.
Listening deeply, man kept faith with the source.

None dreaded judgement.
For no table of crimes measured out
The degrees of torture allotted
Between dismissal and death.
No plaintiff
Prayed in panic to the tyrant's puppet.
Undefended all felt safe and were happy.

Then the great conifers
Ruffled at home on the high hills.
They had no premonition of the axe
Hurtling towards them on its parabola.
Or of the shipyards. Or of what other lands
They would glimpse from the lift of the ocean swell.
No man had crossed salt water.

Cities had not dug themselves in
Behind deep moats, guarded by towers.
No sword had bitten its own
Reflection in the shield. No trumpets
Magnified the battle-cries
Of lions and bulls
Out through the mouth-holes in helmets.

Men needed no weapons.
Nations loved one another.
And the earth, unbroken by plough or by hoe,
Piled the table high. Mankind
Was content to gather the abundance
Of whatever ripened.
Blackberry or strawberry, mushroom or truffle,
Every kind of nut, figs, apples, cherries,
Apricots and pears, and, ankle deep,
Acorns under the tree of the Thunderer.
Spring weather, the airs of spring,
All year long brought blossom.
The unworked earth
Whitened beneath the bowed wealth of the corn.
Rivers of milk mingled with rivers of nectar.
And out of the black oak oozed amber honey.

After Jove had castrated Saturn,
Under the new reign the Age of Silver—
(Lower than the Gold, but better
Than the coming Age of Brass)—
Fell into four seasons.

Now, as never before,
All colour burnt out of it, the air
Wavered into flame. Or icicles
Strummed in the wind that made them.
Not in a cave, not in a half-snug thicket,

[*Creation; Four Ages; Lycaon; Flood*

Not behind a windbreak of wattles,
For the first time
Man crouched under a roof, at a fire.
Now every single grain
Had to be planted
By hand, in a furrow
That had been opened in earth by groaning oxen.

After this, third in order,
The Age of Brass
Brought a brazen people,
Souls fashioned on the same anvil
As the blades their hands snatched up
Before they cooled. But still
Mankind listened deeply
To the harmony of the whole creation,
And aligned
Every action to the greater order
And not to the moment's blind
Apparent opportunity.

Last comes the Age of Iron.
And the day of Evil dawns.
Modesty,
Loyalty,
Truth,
Go up like a mist—a morning sigh off a graveyard.

Snares, tricks, plots come hurrying
Out of their dens in the atom.
Violence is an extrapolation
Of the cutting edge
Into the orbit of the smile.
Now comes the love of gain—a new god
Made out of the shadow

Of all the others. A god who peers
Grinning from the roots of the eye-teeth.

Now sails bulged and the cordage cracked
In winds that still bewildered the pilots.
And the long trunks of trees
That had never shifted in their lives
From some mountain fastness
Leapt in their coffins
From wavetop to wavetop,
Then out over the rim of the unknown.

Meanwhile the ground, formerly free to all
As the air or sunlight,
Was portioned by surveyors into patches,
Between boundary markers, fences, ditches.
Earth's natural plenty no longer sufficed.
Man tore open the earth, and rummaged in her
    bowels.
Precious ores the Creator had concealed
As close to hell as possible
Were dug up—a new drug
For the criminal. So now iron comes
With its cruel ideas. And gold
With crueller. Combined, they bring war—
War, insatiable for the one,
With bloody hands employing the other.
Now man lives only by plunder. The guest
Is booty for the host. The bride's father,
Her heirloom, is a windfall piggybank
For the groom to shatter. Brothers
Who ought to love each other
Prefer to loathe. The husband longs
To bury his wife and she him.
Stepmothers, for the sake of their stepsons,

Study poisons. And sons grieve
Over their father's obdurate good health.
The inward ear, attuned to the Creator,
Is underfoot like a dog's turd. Astraea,
The Virgin
Of Justice—the incorruptible
Last of the immortals—
Abandons the blood-fouled earth.

But not even heaven was safe.
Now came the turn of the giants.
Excited by this human novelty—freedom
From the long sight and hard knowledge
Of divine wisdom—they coveted
The very throne of Jove. They piled to the stars
A ramp of mountains, then climbed it.

Almighty Jove
Mobilised his thunderbolts. That salvo
Blew the top off Olympus,
Toppled the shattered
Pelion off Ossa
And dumped it
Over the giants.
They were squashed like ripe grapes.

Mother Earth, soaked with their blood,
Puddled her own clay in it and created
Out of the sludgy mortar new offspring
Formed like men.

These hybrids were deaf
To the intelligence of heaven. They were revolted
By the very idea
Of a god and sought only

How to kill each other.
The paternal bent for murder alone bred true.

Observing all this from his height
Jove groaned. It reminded him
Of what Lycaon had done at a banquet.
As he thought of that such a fury
Took hold of the Father of Heaven
It amazed even himself.

Then the gods jump to obey
His heaven-shaking summons to council.
The lesser gods come hurrying
From all over the Universe.
They stream along the Milky Way, their highway,
To the Thunderer's throne
Between wide-open halls, ablaze with lights,
Where the chief gods
Are housed in the precincts of Jove's palace
At the very summit of heaven
As in their own shrines.

When the gods had taken their seats
Jove loomed over them,
Leaning on his ivory sceptre.
He swung back his mane
With a movement that jolted
The sea, the continents and heaven itself.
His lips curled from the flame of his anger
As he spoke: "When the giants
Whose arms came in hundreds,
Each of them a separate sea-monster,
Reached for heaven, I was less angered.
Those creatures were dreadful
But they were few—a single family.

Many venomous branches, a single root.
They could be plucked out with a single gesture.
But now, to the ocean's furthest shore,
I have to root out, family by family,
Mankind's teeming millions.
Yet I swear
By the rivers that run through the underworld
This is what I shall do.
You think heaven is safe?
We have a population of demi-gods,
Satyrs, nymphs, fauns, the playful
Spirits of wild places,
Astral entities who loiter about.
When we denied these the freedom of heaven
We compensated them
With their grottoes and crags, their woods and their
    well-springs,
Their dells and knolls. In all these sanctuaries
We should protect them.
Imagine their fears
Since the uncontrollable Lycaon
Plotted against me, and attempted
To do away with me—Jove, King of Heaven,
Whose right hand
Rests among thunderheads and whose left
Sways the assemblies of heaven!"

The gods roared their outrage.
They shouted
For instant correction
Of this madman.
Just as when those gangsters
Tried to wash out Rome's name
With Caesar's blood,
Mankind recoiled stunned

As at the world's ending and
The very air hallucinated horrors.

O Augustus, just as you see now
The solicitude of all your people
So did the Father of Heaven
Survey that of the gods.

Just so, too, the majesty of Jove
Quieted heaven with a gesture.
"This crime," he told them,
"Has been fully punished. What it was
And how I dealt with it, now let me tell you.
The corruption of mankind
Rose to my nostrils, here in heaven,
As a stench of putrid flesh.
Seeking better news of the species
I left Olympus, and in the shape of a man
Walked the earth.
If I were to recount, in every detail,
How man has distorted himself
With his greed, his lies, his indifference,
The end of time, I think,
Would overtake the reckoning.
Alerted as I was
I was still unprepared for what I found.
I had crossed Maenalus—
The asylum of lions and bears.
I had passed Cyllene
And the shaggy heights and gorges
Of freezing Lycaeus.
At nightfall
I came to the unwelcoming hearth
Of the Arcadian King.
I revealed, with a sign,

The presence of a god.
But when the whole court
Fell to the ground and worshipped,
King Lycaon laughed.
He called them credulous fools.
'The simplest of experiments,' he snarled,
'Will show us whether this guest of ours
Is the mighty god he wants us to think him
Or some common rascal. Then the truth
Will stare us all in the face.'

"Lycaon's demonstration
Was to be the shortest of cuts.
He planned to come to my bed, where I slept that
        night,
And kill me.
But he could not resist embellishing
His little test
With one introductory refinement.

"Among his prisoners, as a hostage,
Was a Molossian. Lycaon picked this man,
Cut his throat, bled him, butchered him
And while the joints still twitched
Put some to bob in a stew, the rest to roast.

"The moment
He set this mess in front of me on the table
I acted.
With a single thunderbolt
I collapsed his palazzo.
One bang, and the whole pile came down
Onto the household idols and jujus
That this monster favoured.
The lightning had gone clean through Lycaon.
His hair was in spikes.

Somehow he staggered
Half-lifted by the whumping blast
Out of the explosion.
Then out across open ground
Trying to scream. As he tried
To force out screams
He retched howls.
His screams
Were vomited howls.
Trying to shout to his people
He heard only his own howls.
Froth lathered his lips.
Then the blood-thirst, natural to him,
Went insane.
From that moment
The Lord of Arcadia
Runs after sheep. He rejoices
As a wolf starved near death
In a frenzy of slaughter.
His royal garments, formerly half his wealth,
Are a pelt of jagged hair.
His arms are lean legs.
He has become a wolf.

"But still his humanity clings to him
And suffers in him.
The same grizzly mane,
The same black-ringed, yellow,
Pinpoint-pupilled eyes, the same
Demented grimace. His every movement possessed
By the same rabid self.

"So one house is destroyed.
But one only. Through the whole earth
Every roof
Is the den of a Lycaon.

In this universal new religion
All are fanatics—suckled
Not by the sweet wisdom of heaven
But by a wolf. All adore, all worship
Greed, cruelty, the Lycaon
In themselves. All are guilty.
Therefore all must be punished. I have spoken."

As he ended, one half the gods
Added their boom of approval
To his rage. The other deepened it
With solid and silent assent.
All were quietly appalled
To imagine mankind annihilated.
What would heaven do
With a globeful of empty temples?
Altars attended
Only by spiders? Was earth's beauty
Henceforth to be judged
Solely by the single-minded
Palates of wild beasts
And returned to the worm
Because man had failed?

God comforted the gods.
If everything was left to him, he promised,
He could produce a new humanity—
Different from the first model and far
More prudently fashioned.

So now Jove set his mind to the deletion
Of these living generations. He pondered
Mass electrocution by lightning.
But what if the atoms ignited,
What if a single ladder of flame
Rushing up through the elements

Reduced heaven to an afterglow? Moreover,
God as he was, he knew
That earth's and heaven's lease for survival
Is nothing more than a lease.
That both must fall together—
The globe and its brightness combined
Like a tear
Or a single bead of sweat—
Into the bottomless fires of the first, last forge.

Afraid that he might just touch off that future
With such weapons, forged in that same smithy,
He reversed his ideas.
He dipped his anger in the thought of water.
Rain, downpour, deluge, flood—these
Could drown the human race, and be harmless.

In a moment he had withdrawn the blast
That fixes the Northern ice.
He tethered the parching winds
Off mountains and out of deserts
That bare the flaring blue and crack lips.
He gave the whole earth to the South Wind.
Darkening into the East, and into the West,
Two vast wings of water opened. One
Thunderhead filled heaven,
Feathered with darkness, bringing darkness
From below the Equator.
The face of this South Wind, as he came,
Boiled with squalling tempest.
Beard and hair were a whorl of hurricanes.
He dragged whole oceans up, like a peacock shawl.
And as he drubbed and wrung the clouds
Between skyfuls of fist, quaking the earth,
Shocks of thunder dumped the floods.
Juno's messenger, the rainbow,

Swept from earth to heaven, topping up the darkness.
Every crop was flattened. The farmer's year
Of labour dissolved as he wept.

But still there was not water enough in heaven
To satisfy Jove's fury.
So Neptune, his brother, god of the seas,
Brought up tidal waves,
And assembled every river
There in the bottom of the ocean
And ordered them to open their aquifers
Ignoring all confines.
The rivers raced back to their sources
And erupted.
Neptune himself harpooned the earth with his trident.
Convulsed, it quaked open
Crevasse beneath crevasse
Disgorging the subterranean waters.

Now flood heaps over flood.
Orchards, crops, herds, farms are scooped up
And sucked under
By the overland maelstrom.
Temples and their statues liquefy
Kneeling into the swirls.
Whatever roof or spire or turret
Resists the rip of currents
Goes under the climbing levels.
Till earth and sea seem one—a single sea
Without a shore.
A few crowds are squeezed on diminishing islets
Of hill-tops.
Men are rowing in circles aimlessly, crazed,
Where they ploughed straight furrows or steered
    wagons.
One pitches a sail over corn.

Another steers his keel
Over his own chimney.
One catches a fish in the top of an elm.
Anchors drag over grazing
Or get a grip under vine roots.
Where lean goats craned for brown tufts
Fat seals gambol over and under each other.

The Nereids roam astounded
Through submerged gardens,
Swim in silent wonder into kitchens,
Touch the eyes of marble busts that gaze
Down long halls, under the wavering light.

Dolphins churn through copses.
Hunting their prey into oak trees, they shake out acorns
That sink slowly.
Wolves manage awhile,
Resting their heads on drowned and floating sheep.
Lions ride exhausted horses. Tigers
Try to mount foundering bullocks.
The strong stag's fine long legs,
Growing weedier, tangle in undercurrents.
The wild boar, the poor swimmer, soon goes under.
Even his faithful heavy defenders,
The thunderbolt and lightning-flash of his tusks,
Have joined the weight against him.
Birds grow tired of the air.
The ocean, with nowhere else to go,
Makes its bed in the hills,
Pulling its coverlet over bare summits.

While starvation picks off the survivors.

Drowned mankind, imploring limbs outspread,
Floats like a plague of dead frogs.

Phaethon

When Phaethon bragged about his father, Phoebus
The sun-god,
His friends mocked him. "Your mother must be crazy
Or you're crazy to believe her.
How could the sun be anybody's father?"

In a rage of humiliation
Phaethon came to his mother, Clymene.
"They're all laughing at me,
And I can't answer. What can I say? It's horrible.
I have to stand like a dumb fool and be laughed at.

"If it's true, Mother," he cried, "if the sun,
The high god Phoebus, if he is my father,
Give me proof.
Give me evidence that I belong to heaven."
Then he embraced her. "I beg you,

"On my life, on your husband Merops' life,
And on the marriage hopes of my sisters,
Only give me proof that the sun is my father."
Either moved by her child's distress,
Or piqued to defend her honour against the old
     rumour,

Clymene responded. She stretched her arms to the
     sun:

"By the dazzling ball itself
Who is watching us now, and is listening
To everything I say, I swear
You are his child. You are the son

"Of that great star which lights up the whole world.
If I lie, then I pray
To go blind, this moment,
And never again to see the light of day.
But if you want so much to meet your father

"It is not impossible.
He rises from that land beyond our borders.
If you must have the truth about yourself
Go and ask him for it."
Phaethon

Rushed out, his head ablaze
With the idea of heaven.
He crossed his own land, Ethiopia,
Then India, that trembled in the sun's nearness,
And came to his father's dawn palace.

Fittingly magnificent
Columns underpropped a mass
Of gold strata so bright
The eyes flinched from it.
The whole roof a reflector
Of polished ivory.
The silver doors like sheet flame—
And worked into that flame
Vulcan, the god of fire,
Had set, in relief, a portrait of the Creation.
There were the seas. Triton
Cruising in foam, through the swell,
Making his lonely music.

And Proteus, amoebic,
Flitting from form to form,
A submarine, shape-shifting shadow.
And Aegeon, half-reclining,
His arms across two whales.
Doris was there with her daughters—
Swimming, riding fishes,
Or sitting on rocks and combing their hair.
Each one quite different
Yet all looking like sisters.
And there, on earth, were the cities, the people,
The woods, the beasts, the rivers, the nymphs
And the spirits of wild places.
Surrounding the whole thing, the Zodiac—
On the right door six signs, and six on the left.

Phaethon climbed the steep approach
And entered the house of his father
Who had brought him so much shame.
He went straight in to the royal presence—
But had to stand back: the huge light was so fierce
He could not go near it.
For there was the god—Phoebus, the sun,
Robed in purple
And sitting on a throne of emeralds
That blazed,
Splitting and refracting his flames.
To right and left of him
His annual retinue stood arrayed—
The seasons, the generations, and the Hours.
Spring, crowned with a flower garland. Summer,
Naked but for a coronet of ripe corn.
Autumn, purple from treading the wine-press.
And Winter, shivering in rags,
His white hair and his beard
Jagged with icicles.

The boy stared dumbfounded,
Dazed by the marvel of it all.
Then the great god
Turned on him the gaze that misses nothing
And spoke: "Phaethon, my son!

"Yes, I call you my child—or rather, a man
A father might be proud of. Why are you here?
You must have come with a purpose. What is it?"
Phaethon replied: "O God, Light of Creation!
O Phoebus, my father—if I may call you father!—

"If Clymene is not protecting herself
From some shame by claiming your name for me
Give me the solid proof.
Let it be known to the whole world
That I am your son. Remove all doubt."

His father doffed his crown of blinding light
And, beckoning Phaethon closer, embraced him.
"Do not fear to call me father.
Your mother told you the truth.
To free yourself from doubt—ask me for something.

"Anything, I promise you shall have it.
And though I have never seen the lake in hell
By which we gods in heaven make our oaths
Inviolable, I call on that lake now
To witness this oath of mine."

Phoebus had barely finished before Phaethon
Asked for the chariot of the sun
And one whole day driving the winged horses.
His father recoiled. He almost
Cursed his own oath. His head shook

As if it were trying to break its promise.
"Your foolish words," he said,
"Show me the tragic folly of mine.
If promises could be broken
I would break this. I would deny you nothing

"Except this. Be persuaded
The danger of what you ask is infinite—
To yourself, to the whole Creation.
The forces, the materials, the laws
Of all Creation are balanced

"On the course of that chariot and those horses.
A boy could not hope to control them.
You are my son, but mortal. No mortal
Could hope to manage those reins.
Not even the gods are allowed to touch them.

"Only see how foolish you are.
The most conceited of the gods
Knows better
Than to dream he could survive
One day riding the burning axle-tree.

"Yes, even Jupiter
High god of all heaven, whose hand
Cradles the thunderbolt—
He keeps his fingers off those reins.
And who competes with him?

"Our first stretch is almost vertical.
Fresh as they are, first thing,
It is all the horses can do to get up it.
Then on to mid-heaven. Terrifying
To look down through nothing

"At earth and sea, so tiny.
My heart nearly struggles out of my body
As the chariot sways.
Then the plunge towards evening—
There you need strength on the reins. Tethys,

"Who waits to receive me
Into her waters, is always afraid
I shall topple—
And come tumbling
Head over heels in a tangled mass.

"Remember, too,
That the whole sky is revolving
With its constellations, its planets.
I have to force my course against that—
Not to be swept backwards as all else is.

"What will you do,
Your feet braced in the chariot, the reins in your
        hands,
When you have to counter the pull
Of the whirling Poles? When the momentum
Of the whole reeling cosmos hauls you off sideways?

"Maybe you expect
To come across delectable cities of the gods,
Groves and temples beautifully appointed,
Much as on earth. It is not like that.
Instead, benighted gulches, with monsters.

"Even if you were able to stick to the route
You have to pass
The horns of the Great Bull, the nasty arrows
Of the Haemonian Archer, the gaping jaw
Of the infuriated Lion,

"And the Scorpion's lifted spike, its pincers
That grab for you from one side while the Crab
Rushes at you with its double crushers
From the other.
And how could you cope with the horses?

"Even for me
It is not easy, once they are fired up
With the terrible burners
That they stoke in their deep chests
And that belch flames from their mouths and nostrils.

"Once their blood is up
They will hardly obey me, and they know me.
Think again. Do not ask me
For what will destroy you.
You ask me for solid proof that you are my son:

"My fears for your life are proof, solid enough.
Look at me. If only your eyes
Could see through to my heart and see it
Sick with a father's distress.
Choose anything else in Creation—it is yours.

"But this one thing you have chosen—
I dare not grant it. Choose again, Phaethon.
You have asked me not for an honour, as you suppose,
But for a punishment. O my son,
This is no honour, this is a punishment.

"You throw your arms around my neck and persist.
You have no notion of what you are asking for.
But I have sworn by Styx and you shall have
Whatever you desire. Only, my son,
Ask again, for something different, wiser."

Phaethon seemed not to have heard.
He wanted nothing but to drive
The chariot and horses of the sun.
His father could find no other means to delay him.
He led him out to the chariot.

Vulcan had made it. The axle-tree was gold,
And the chariot-pole gold. The wheel-rims were gold.
The wheel-spokes silver. The harness, collar and traces,
Crusted with chrysolites and other jewels,
Blazed in the beams of the sun-god.

And as Phaethon stood there, light-headed with
    confidence,
Giddy with admiration
Of the miraculous workmanship and detail,
Dawn opened her purple doors behind him,
Letting the roses spill from her chambers.

The stars decamped—their vanishing detachments
Supervised by the morning star
Who followed them last.
When the sun-god saw that, and the reddening sky
And the waning moon seeming to thaw

He called the Hours to yoke the horses.
The light-footed goddesses brought them
Swinging in steam from the high stables,
Blowing soft flames, fat with ambrosia.
Yoked to the chariot, they champed at the jangling
    bits.

But now as Phoebus anointed Phaethon
With a medicinal blocker
To protect him from the burning

And fixed the crown of rays on the boy's head
He saw the tragedy to come

And sighed: "At least, if you can,
Stick to these instructions, my son.
First: use the whip not at all, or lightly.
But rein the team hard. It is not easy.
Their whole inclination is to be gone.

"Second: avoid careering
Over the whole five zones of heaven.
Keep to the broad highway that curves
Within the three zones, temperate and tropic.
Avoid the Poles, and their killing blizzards.

"Keep to that highway, follow the wheel ruts.
Share your heat fairly
Between heaven and earth, not too low
And not crashing in among the stars. Too high,
You will set heaven aflame—and, too low, earth.

"The middle way is best, and safest.
And do not veer too far to the right
Where your wheels might crush the Serpent, nor to
       the left
Where they might be shattered against the Altar.
Take a bearing between them.

"Now Fortune go with you. And I pray
She will take care of you better
Than you have taken care of yourself.
We have talked too long. Night has gone down
Behind the world westward. No more delays.

"Our great light is looked for.

"Grasp the reins. Or better, with a changed mind,
While your feet are still on the earth,
Before you have hurled your idiot emulation
Among the terrors of space,
Grasp my advice.

"Leave my chariot to me.
Let me give the world the light it expects,
A light for you to smile at in safety."
But Phaethon, too drunk with his youth to listen,
Ignored the grieving god

And leapt aboard, and catching the reins
From his father's hands, joyfully thanked him.
Pyrois, Eous, Aethon, Phlegon—
The four winged horses stormed to be off.
Their whinnyings quaked the air-waves,

A writhing crackle of interference
Throughout heaven. And their pawing hooves
Racketed at the barred gate.
Then Tethys (who knew nothing
Of the part about to be played by her grandson)
Lifted the bars—and all space
Lay open to the racers.

They burst upwards, they hurled themselves
Ahead of themselves,
Winged hooves churning cloud.
They outstripped those dawn winds from the East—
But from the first moment
They felt something wrong with the chariot.
The load was too light.
More like a light pinnace
Without ballast or cargo,

Without the deep-keeled weight to hold a course,
Bucking and flipping
At every wave,
Sliding away sidelong at every gust.
The chariot
Bounced and was whisked about as if it were empty.

When the horses felt this
They panicked.
They swerved off the highway
And plunged into trackless heaven.
Their driver, rigid with fear,
Gripped the chariot rail. It was true,
He had neither the strength nor the skill
To manage those reins.
And even if he could have controlled
The wild heads of the horses
He did not know the route.

For the first time
The stars of the Plough smoked.
And though the Arctic Ocean
Was forbidden to them they strained
To quench themselves in it.

And the Serpent
That hibernated close to the Pole Star
Harmless, and inert in the cold, woke
Scorched, lashing, furious to cool itself.

Even slow Boötes puffed and scrambled
To get away from the heat,
Dragging his plough like an anchor.

And now Phaethon looked down
From the zenith—

And saw the earth
So far below, so terrifyingly tiny,
His whole body
Seemed suddenly bloodless.
His knees wobbled, his eyes
Dazzled and darkened.
He wished he had never seen his father's horses.
He wished he had never learned
Who his father was. He wished his father
Had broken his promise.
He wanted only to be known
As the son of Merops.

Meanwhile the chariot bounded along
Like a ship under a gale
When seas have smashed the rudder
And the ropes have gone
And the helmsman
Crouches and clings in the scuppers,
And prays,
Hiding his eyes with his arm.

What could he do?
Much of the sky was behind him,
But always more ahead.
He looked East, trying to measure
What he had covered.
He looked West—where his Fate lay waiting.
Either way, nothing could help him.

His wrists were looped in the reins he no longer
Had the strength to cling to.
Even the horses' names had gone out of his head.

And now he saw the monsters
Littered among the constellations.

[*Phaethon*

The Scorpion loomed,
Suspending his tail
Over the wide embrace of his claws,
Sprawling across two signs of the Zodiac.

When Phaethon saw that, when he saw
The ponderous talon of the sting, bulbed with poison,
He dropped the reins.
They fell in a tangle over the horses.
Then the horses took off, blindly.
Uncontrolled, they let their madness
Fling them this way and that
All over the sky.
They dashed in among the stars
Switching the chariot along
Like a whip-tail.
They swept low—till the clouds boiled in their wake
And the moon was astonished
To see her brother's chariot below her.

Earth began to burn, the summits first.
Baked, the cracks gaped. All fields, all thickets,
All crops were instant fuel—
The land blazed briefly.
In the one flare noble cities
Were rendered
To black stumps of burnt stone.
Whole nations, in all their variety,
Were clouds of hot ashes, blowing in the wind.
Forest-covered mountains were bonfires.
Athos burned.
Cilician Taurus and Tmolus,
Oeta and Ida, formerly blessed for its springs,
Helicon, home of the Muses, all burned.
And Haemus, that Orpheus would make famous.
The twin peaks of Parnassus, and Cynthus and Eryx,

Were pillars of fire. Etna convulsed
In multiple eruptions.
The snows of Rhodope
Boiled off, and the ridges glowed.
Othrys, Mimas, Dindyma, Mycale
And Cithaeron, dancing place of the Bassarids,
Were ablaze.
Scythia's freezing winds could not protect it.
Ossa, Pindus, Olympus bigger than either,
The Alps that look across Europe
And the Apennines, their clouds gone,
Burned like fleeces.

Now Phaethon saw the whole world
Mapped with fire. He looked through flames
And he breathed flames.
Flame in and flame out, like a fire-eater.
As the chariot sparked white-hot
He cowered from the showering cinders.
His eyes streamed in the fire-smoke.
And in the boiling darkness
He no longer knew where he was
Or where he was going.
He hung on as he could and left everything
To the horses.

That day, they say,
The Ethiopians were burnt black.
That day,
Libya, in a flash of steam,
Became a shimmering desert,
Where the nymphs of the springs and lakes
Wandered like wraiths, wailing for lost water.
Boeotia wept for the fountain of Dirce,
Argos for Amymone, Ephyre for Pirene.
Strong rivers fared no better.

The shallows of Tanais fried. Old Peneus,
Mysian Caicus and the headlong Ismenus—
Their shallows and riffles bubbled as if over pebbles
That were red-hot.
And Trojan Xanthus, who would be burned again.
Yellow Lycormas poured a reeking soup.
Looped Meander steamed like a scalded serpent.
Melas in Thrace, Eurotas in Sparta,
Euphrates in Babylon,
Orontes, Thermodon, Ganges, Phasis and Hister
Seemed to smoulder in their beds.
Alpheus dived through fire. Sperchius
Crept between banks that broke into flame.
The gold in Tagus melted.
The singing swans of Cayster
Cried in dismay as the river boiled,
Scalding and stripping their plumage.
The terrified Nile
Escaped into Africa, and hid his head
Among smouldering mountains, leaving the seven
Delta channels
To blow into dunes.
Ismarus' bed was a gully of burning dust.
The Rhine, the Rhône, the Po and the Tiber
Which had been promised an Empire
Were bubbling pits of quag in scabby trenches.
The earth cracked open. And the unnatural light
Beamed down into hell
Scaring the king and queen of that kingdom
With their own terrific shadows.
The seas shrank, baring deserts.
Submarine mountains emerged as islands,
Multiplying the Cyclades.
Fish hugged the bottom of their deepest holes.
Seals bobbed belly up, lifeless.
And the dolphins stayed far down.

Three times
Neptune reared his angry head and shoulders
Above the bubbling surface
And each time plunged again
To escape the searing flames of the air.

Then the Goddess of Earth
Alarmed by the waters crowding into her bowels
Pushed up through the embers
And lifted her head and neck into the furnace.

She spread her hand
To shield her face from the sun.
The terror
That shook her body shook the whole earth.
She crouched lower and cried
With her holy voice:
"You God of the gods,
If my annihilation
Has been decided, why drag it out?
Where are your thunderbolts
To finish the whole thing quickly?
If I am to end in fire
Let it be your fire, O God,
That would redeem it a little.
I can hardly speak."
She choked in a squall of ashes.
"See my hair singed to the roots,
My eyes cauterised by your glare.
Are these my reward
For my fertility, my limitless bounty,
My tireless production?
Is this my compensation
For undergoing the ploughshare,
The pick and the mattock,
My flesh gouged and attacked and ground to a tilth

Year in year out? Is this how you pay me
For foddering fat beasts,
For plumping the milky grain that suckles man,
For concocting the essences and rich herbs
That smoke on your altars?
Even if I have somehow deserved all this
How are the seas guilty, or your brother?
Why should the oceans, that are his portion,
Cringe and shrink from the sky?
But if you are deaf to us
What about your own heaven? Look at it.
Both Poles are glowing. Once they go
Your whole realm flies off its axle,
Your palace is rubbish in space.
And look at Atlas. He is in trouble.
His shoulders are fabulous, but who can carry
The incineration of a Universe?"

Then heat overcame her. Little by little
She drew in her smoking head,
Like a tortoise, and sank into herself—
Into the caves, close to the land of ghosts.

The Almighty, aroused,
Called on the gods,
Including Phoebus who had lent the chariot—
He asked them to witness
That heaven and earth could be saved only
By what he now must do.
He soared to the top of heaven,
Into the cockpit of thunder.
From here he would pour the clouds
And roll the thunders and hurl bolts.
But now he was cloudless—
There was not a drop of rain in all heaven.

With a splitting crack of thunder he lifted a bolt,
Poised it by his ear,
Then drove the barbed flash point-blank into
    Phaethon.
The explosion
Snuffed the ball of flame
As it blew the chariot to fragments. Phaethon
Went spinning out of his life.

The crazed horses scattered.
They tore free, with scraps of the yoke,
Trailing their broken reins.
The wreckage fell through space,
Shattered wheels gyrating far apart,
Shards of the car, the stripped axle,
Bits of harness—all in slow motion
Sprinkled through emptiness.

Phaethon, hair ablaze,
A fiery speck, lengthening a vapour trail,
Plunged towards the earth
Like a star
Falling and burning out on a clear night.

In a remote land
Far from his home
The hot current
Of the broad Eridanus
Quenched his ember—
And washed him ashore.
The Italian nymphs
Buried his remains, that were glowing again
And flickering little flames
Of the three-forked fire from God.
Over his grave, on a rock they wrote this:

Here lies Phoebus' boy who died
In the sun's chariot.
His strength too human, and too hot
His courage and his pride.

His father mourned, hidden,
Eclipsed with sorrow.
They say no sun showed on that day.
But the fires of the burning earth
Were so far useful, to give some light.
And now Clymene's outcry
Equalled the catastrophe.
Mad with grief, she searched the whole earth
To find the boy's limbs, or his bones.
She came to the grave. With her breasts naked
She embraced the engraved rock.

The daughters of the sun grieved as keenly,
Beating their breasts,
Throwing themselves down on their brother's tomb,
Calling incessantly
For the one who would never hear them.
Days, weeks, months, they mourned.
Their lamentations were obsessive,
As if they could never exhaust them
They wore out four full moons with their wailings
Until at last Phaethusa—
As she flung herself to the ground—
Cried out that her feet were fixed of a sudden.
And Lampetie, as she stepped to help her,
Found her own feet rooted, immovable.

A third, tearing her hair,
Brought away handfuls of leaves.
One screamed that a tree bole
Had imprisoned her calves and thighs.

Another was whimpering with horror
To find her arms crooking into stiff branches.
And as they all struggled in vain
To escape or understand, tree bark,
Rough and furrowed, crept on upwards
Over their bodies, throats, faces—
Till it left only their lips, human enough
To call for their mother.

And what could she do
But stagger to and fro
In growing terror—
Torn this way and that,
Kissing the mouths she could still find?
And when she tried to free her daughters,
Ripping at the bark, and snapping the branches—
A liquid, like blood,
Came welling out of the wounds,
And the mouths screamed:
"O Mother, do not hurt us.
Though we are trees
We are your daughters—
Oh, now we must leave you."

So their last words were silenced
By the sealing bark.
But then, through that bark,
There oozed lymph like tears, that in the sun's light
Solidified as amber.
These dropped from the boughs
Into the hurrying river
Which carried them off
To adorn, some day far in the future,
Roman brides.

Callisto and Arcas

After Phaethon's disaster
Jove was repairing the earth,
Clothing the burnt lands again with life—

But even such a labour of love,
So urgent, has to yield
To one even more urgent.

And there she was—the Arcadian beauty, Callisto.
He stared. Lust bristled up his thighs
And poured into the roots of his teeth.

She wasn't the sort
That sat at home, her eyes in a daze
On the whirl of a spinning wheel, or a mirror.

She loped along with the huntress Diana,
Her tunic pinned with a bold brooch,
Her ponytail in a white ribbon

And in her hand a bow or a javelin.
Of all Maenalus' nymphs she was Diana's
Favourite. But favourites have to fall.

The sun was well past noon when this girl
Came in under the massive cooling columns
Of a virgin forest. She slackened her bow

And setting her quiver as a pillow
Flung herself down among the anemones
On the sun-littered floor of the woodland.

And that is where Jupiter spotted her.
Defenceless, drowsing, languid. "A wonder!"
He breathed, "that my wife need never disturb,

"Or if she happens to, the price will be worth it."
Callisto woke to a voice. Above her
Diana's perfect double, gazing down,

Was speaking to her: "Best-loved of all my virgins,
Where did you hunt today? On which ridges,
Down which valleys?" The girl sat up, astonished—

"O Goddess, O my divine mistress—
Greater than Jupiter—
And I don't care if he hears me—" Jove smiled

Secretly behind his disguise
Delighted to receive more adulation
Than himself. He stretched beside her and kissed her,

A kiss more than maidenly, that roughened—
A kiss that, as she tried to answer him,
Gagged her voice, while his arms tightened round her,

Straitjacketing her body, and his action
Revealed
The god—irresistible and shameless.

Callisto's piety had limits.
She fought. If Juno had seen how she fought
Her final cruelty might have been modified.

But it was no good. Desperately as she denied him
The God of gods went off home contented
As if from heavenly bliss to heavenly bliss.

The girl wept. Suddenly, she hated the forest,
The flowers, that had watched while it happened.
She was in such a hurry to get away

She almost abandoned her bow and her quiver.
Diana, coming along the ridge of Maenalus
With her virgin troop, after hard hunting,

Saw her darling, and called her. Callisto's
Jumpy terror of Diana's likeness
Grabbed with electric hands, and she bolted—

But then recognised her friends, the virgins
Who ran with the goddess,
And knew this could not be Jove. So she joined them.

But changed now. How hard it is
To keep guilt out of the face!
She no longer led the troop—

Was no longer the boisterous nearest
To the goddess. She hung back, eyes to the ground,
As if slinking along from hiding to hiding.

If any spoke to her she blushed, then paled.
Without her divinity Diana
Could not have missed the thousand human tokens

That were no puzzle to the nymphs.
Nine months passed. Finally came the day,
Heated with hunting under the hot sun

Diana led her company into a grove
With a cool stream over smooth pebbles.
"Here is a place," she called,

"Where we can strip and bathe and be unseen."
The Arcadian girl was in a panic.
The rest were naked in no time—she delayed,

She made excuses. Then all the others
Stripped her by force—and with shrill voices
Exclaimed at her giveaway belly

That she tried pitifully to hide
With her hands. The goddess, outraged,
Cried: "Do not defile this water or us.

"Get away from us now and for ever."
Meanwhile, Juno had seen everything.
She was merely waiting for an occasion

To exact the exemplary punishment.
The moment Jove's bastard was born—
A boy, Arcas!—her fury exploded.

She stared in wild hatred at the new infant.
"So," she screamed at Callisto, "the world can see
You have perfected your insult—and my shame.

"Now see me perfect my revenge
On this beauty of yours
That so unbalanced my husband."

She grabbed the girl by the hair
Above her forehead, and jerked her down flat on her
        face.
As Callisto lay there, pleading for mercy

With outstretched arms—those arms the god had
     caressed
Suddenly bushed thick with black hair,
Her hands curved into scoops of long talons—

They had become feet. And her mouth
That Jupiter had kissed in his rapture
Was fanged jaws, like a torn open wound.

Then to empty her cries of their appeal
The goddess nipped off her speech. Instead of words
A shattering snarl burst from her throat, a threat—

Callisto was a bear.
Yet her mind was unaltered. Her lament
Was the roar of a bear—but her grief was human.

And though they were a bear's forepaws
That she raked at heaven's face with,
Her despair over Jove's ingratitude,

Though she could not speak it, was a girl's.
Afraid of sleeping in the woods, she crept into the
     gardens
Of what had been her home.

Often she galloped for her life
Hearing the hounds. Often she laboured, gasping,
Hunted across the hillsides where she had hunted.

Sometimes she forgot what she was
And hid from the other creatures. As before—
Above all, what this bear feared were the bears.

She also feared the wolves,
Though her own father
Was out there among them, one of them.

Meanwhile, Arcas grew to his fifteenth year.
He knew nothing at all
About his mother. Hunting was his passion.

One day, after choosing the ground carefully,
Reckoning with the wind
And with the lie of the land,

Arcas had pitched his nets
Among the scrubby coverts of Erymanthus.
As he started the drive, of a sudden

Out of the long grass his mother
Reared upright to face him,
Standing tall to see him better, fearless,

As if she recognised him. She recognised him.
Arcas backed slowly, mouth dry,
Terror, three parts wisdom, staring

Fixedly at the eyes that stared at him.
But when she dropped on all fours
And he saw her shaggy shoulders

Humping through undergrowth towards him
He could not think what this great beast intended
If not to kill him. He braced himself

Behind his spear
To meet her momentum
And drive that long, keen-ground blade as deeply

Into her body as he could. Jupiter
Saw it all. He stooped down from heaven
And blocked the bronze point with his finger-tip.

Then spun mother and son up in a whirlwind.
So these two, about to be reunited
In that bloody crime and tragic error,

Found themselves far out in space, transformed
To constellations, the Great Bear and the Small,
Dancing around the Pole Star together.

The Rape
of Proserpina

Ceres was the first
To split open the grassland with a ploughshare.
The first
To plant corn and nurse harvests.
She was the first to give man laws.

Everything man has he owes to Ceres.
So now I sing of her
And so I pray my song may be worthy
Of this great goddess,
For surely she is worthy of the song.

The giant Typhon, that upstart who had dared
To hope for a home in heaven,
Felt his strength returning. He stirred,
Squashed
Under the massive slab of Sicily.

His right hand, reaching towards Rome,
Was crushed under Pelorus,
His left hand under Pachynus,
His legs under Lilybaeum
And his enormous head under Etna.

Flat on his back, he vomited ashes,
Flame, lava, sulphur. His convulsions
Shrugged off cities,

Quaked mountains to rubble.
The whole of Sicily trembled.

The Lord of Hell was aghast to see bedrock
Heaving in waves, like ocean. He looked upwards
For earth's crust to come caving in
Letting the sunglare into hell's glooms,
Dazzling the spectres. Anxious

In a black chariot, behind black horses,
The King of Terrors
Thundered up
To reconnoitre the roof of his kingdom.
He scrutinised the island's foundations,

Double-checked every crevasse, crack, fault,
For sign of a shift.
Probed every weak spot with his sceptre
Tapping rocks and analysing echoes.
Everything seemed to be sound

And he began to feel better. It was then
Aphrodite, sitting on her mountain,
Noticed him.
She woke her winged boy, embraced him, kissed him.
"My child," she whispered, "you who are all my
       power,

"You who are my arms, my hands, my magic,
Bend your bow, my darling,
And sink your shaft, which never missed a challenge,
Into the heart of that god
Who rules hell.

"The deities of the upper world are yours
Whenever you please. Even great Jupiter—

Like a helpless figment of your fancy—
Whatever folly you plot, he will perform it.
The gods of the sea, no less,

"Dance to your prompting arrows, your spurs,
Your goads, your tickling barbs.
That great earth-shaker, Neptune,
Is no more than your trophy.
Over all these your rule is hardly questioned.

"It is time to expand our empire, my child,
Into that third realm—the underworld.
A third of Creation—there for the taking.
Heaven mocks our forbearance, and exploits it.
Your power is less than it was, and mine too.

"I have lost Pallas
And the great huntress Diana—both gone.
And now Ceres' daughter, Proserpina,
Wants to stay a virgin. Do we permit it?
Now is your opportunity.

"If you have any pride in our dominion
Fasten that goddess and her grim uncle
Together with one bolt."
Even as he listened to his mother
Cupid's fingers found the very arrow

For the job—one in a thousand—
True as a ray of the sun tipped with a photon.
He set the soles of his feet to the belly of the bow
And hauling the fletched notch to his chin dimple
Buried it in the dark heart of Pluto.

Near Enna's walls is a deep lake
Known as Pergusa.

The swans on that surface make a music
Magical as the songs
On the swift currents of Cayster.
Trees encircling it
Knit their boughs to protect it
From the sun's flame.
Their leaves nurse a glade of cool shade
Where it is always spring, with spring's flowers.

Proserpina was playing in that glade
With her companions.
Brilliant as butterflies
They flitted hither and thither excitedly
Among lilies and violets. She was heaping
The fold of her dress with the flowers,
Hurrying to pick more, to gather most,
Piling more than any of her friends into baskets.
There the Lord of Hell suddenly saw her.
In the sweep of a single glance
He fell in love
And snatched her away—
Love pauses for nothing.

Terrified, she screamed for her mother,
And screamed to her friends. But louder
And again and again to her mother.
She ripped her frock from her throat downwards—
So all her cherished flowers scattered in a shower.
Then in her childishness
She screamed for her flowers as they fell,
While her ravisher leaped with her
Into his chariot, shouting to the horses
Each one by name,
Whipping their necks with the reins, like the start of a
        race,

And they were off. They were gone—
Leaving the ripped turf and the shocked faces.

Over deep lakes they went,
And over the fumaroles of the Palici
Where reeking pools boil sulphur.
Past the walled stronghold
Of the Bacchiae, who came from Corinth
And built their city
Between a large and a small harbour.

Near Cyane and Pisaean Arethusa
Jagged headlands clasp a narrow cove
Named after Cyane, who lives there—
Among all Sicily's nymphs the most famous.
Cyane
Reared from the water to her waist
And recognised Proserpina.
"You have gone too far, Pluto," she cried.
"You cannot be son-in-law to Ceres
If she does not want you.
You should not have kidnapped this child
But asked for her hand according to custom.
The comparison is remote
But I was loved by Anapus.
He did not carry me off in a violent passion.
He never alarmed me. He was gentle.
And after a courtship of prayers
I was willingly won."

Cyane stretched her arms as she spoke,
To block the path of the horses.
Then the son of Saturn, in a fury,
Plunged his royal sceptre
Down through the bed of her pool

And called to his savage horses.
The bottom of the pool split wide open,
And they dived—
Horses, chariot, Pluto and his prize—
Straight into hell.

Cyane bewailed the rape of the goddess
And the violation of her fountain.
She wept over these wrongs
In secret, as if her heart
Were weeping its blood.
Nothing could comfort her.
Gradually, her sorrow
Melted her into the very waters
Of which she had been the goddess.
Her limbs thinned, her bones became pliant,
Her nails softened. Swiftly she vanished
Into flowing water—first
Her slighter parts, her hair, fingers,
Feet, legs, then her shoulders,
Her back, her breasts, her sides, and at last
No longer blood but clear simple water
Flowed through her veins, and her whole body
Became clear simple water. Nothing remained
To hold or kiss but a twisting current of water.

In despair
Ceres ransacked the earth.
No dawn sodden with dew
Ever found her resting. The evening star
Never found her weary.

She had torn up two pine trees,
Kindled both in Etna,
And holding them high

Through the long nights
Lit her path of glittering frost.

When the sun rose to console her,
Melting the stars, she strode on—
From rising to setting seeking her daughter.
But fatigue and, worse than fatigue, thirst,
Finally overtook her.

Looking for a stream, she found a cottage.
She knocked and asked for water.
An old woman brought her a drink
Of crushed herbs and barley.
While Ceres drank, a boy stared at her—

A cocky brat, who jeered
And called her a greedy guzzling old witch.
His mouth was still wide, his eyes laughing,
When the whole jugful of broth hit him in the face.
The goddess went on glaring at him

As the speckles of the herbs and barley
Stained into his skin, and his arms
Shrank to legs but skinnier,
His whole bodyful of mischief
Shrank to a shape smaller than a lizard

With a long tail.
The old woman let out a cry
And reached for him, but was frightened to touch him
As he scrambled for cover—
He had become a newt.

The lands and the seas
Across which Ceres roamed

Make too long a list.
Searching the whole earth she found herself
Right back where she had started—Sicily.

And so she came to the fount of Cyane,
Who would have told her everything
But her mouth and tongue were dumb water.
Yet they could convey something.
Proserpina's girdle had fallen

Into the pool. Now Cyane's currents
Rolled this to the surface, floating it
Past the startled eyes of the mother.
It was as if only now
Ceres first heard of her loss.

She ripped her hair out in knots.
She hammered her breasts with her clenched fists.
Yet still she knew nothing
Of where her daughter might be.
She accused every country on earth,

Reproached them all for their ingratitude,
Called them unworthy of their harvests.
Above the rest, she cursed Sicily
That had kept this token of her daughter.
Then she slew man and beast in the furrow

With an instant epidemic, throughout the island.
She broke up the ploughs with her bare hands,
Forbade the fields to bear a crop
Of any kind. She made all seed sterile.
This island, that had boasted its plenty

Throughout the world, lay barren.
As soon as the blade showed green—the grain died.

Floods, heatwaves, and tempests
Sluiced away or dried and blew off the tilth.
The bared seeds were collected by birds.

Whatever managed to grow
Grew clogged and matted
With what nobody wanted—
Briars, thistles, thick, fat, creeping weeds
That defied the farmer.

Then Arethusa, the nymph that Alpheus loved,
Lifted her head from her pool,
Swept back her streaming hair, and called to Ceres:
"Great Mother of earth's harvests,
You who have searched through the whole world

"For your vanished daughter,
You have laboured enough, but have raged too much
Against the earth, which was always loyal to you.
The earth is innocent. If she opened herself
To the ravisher, who struck her so cruelly,

"She was far from willing. I am not defending
My own land. I am from Elis,
Born in Pisa. Though I arrived here
A stranger to Sicily, now I love it
Above all other places.

"This is now the home of Arethusa.
I shall live here for ever. And I beg you,
Goddess, to protect it.
Some day, when you are happier,
There will be time for me to tell you

"Why I left my home, and crossed the seas
To come to Ortygia.

Enough that I roamed through the earth, under the
    earth.
The earth's deepest caves opened a pathway,
Till I came up here—and raising my head

"Recognised the stars I had almost forgotten.
But while I was under the earth
As I slid through the Stygian pool
In the underworld, I felt myself
Reflecting a face that looked down at me.

"It was your Proserpina.
She was not happy. Her face was pinched with fear.
Nevertheless, she was a great queen—
The greatest in that kingdom of spectres.
She is the reigning consort of hell's tyrant."

Ceres seemed to be turning to stone
As she listened.
For a long time she was like stone.
Then her stupor was shattered by a scream of fury
As she leaped into her chariot.

Jupiter was astonished
When she materialised in front of him,
Her hair one wild snarl of disarray,
Her face inflamed and swollen with sobbing,
And her voice hacking at him, attacking:

"She is your daughter—
Not only mine, but yours too—
You have to do something.
If her mother's pleas are powerless
Maybe her father's heart will stir for her.

"Don't love her any the less
For my part in her.
After my long search, our daughter is found.
If you can call it finding to have unearthed her
Where she is lost for ever.

"Only let me have her back now
And I would forgive whoever took her,
Even though not a hair of her were mine.
A bandit, a ruffian, is no husband
For a daughter of Jove."

The high god answered calmly:
"I love our daughter no less than you do.
I am bound to her by blood no less than you are.
But see things as they stand. Let your words
Fit the facts. Is this a theft

"Or an act of love? Once you accept him,
This is a son-in-law to be proud of.
Even if he were worthless
He is still the brother of Jupiter.
As it is, in everything

"He is my equal, only not so lucky
In the lottery
That gave heaven to me and hell to him.
Still, if you are determined to take her from him
You can have her—but on one condition.

"The sole condition—
Fixed by the Fates—
Is this:
She can return to heaven
On condition, hear me, on condition

"That she never tasted hell's food."
Jupiter finished. And Ceres was away
To collect her daughter.
But the Fates stopped her.
Proserpina had eaten something.

Absently straying through Pluto's
Overloaded orchard, she had plucked
A pomegranate. Picked its hard rind open
And sucked the glassy flesh from seven seeds.
Almost nothing, but more than enough.

And she had been observed, as she nibbled,
By Ascalaphus. Orphne,
A nymph well known
In the sunless forest of Avernus,
Impregnated by Acheron, her husband,

Had produced this tell-tale,
Who now blabbed
What he had spied through the leaves,
So closing hell's gates on Proserpina.
The Queen of the Underworld groaned,

Scooped a handful of water
From the infernal river Phlegethon
And throwing it in the face of that babbler
Transformed it to an owl's—
A face all beak and huge eyes.

Ascalaphus fainted.
He came to
Between big brown wings,
His human shape gone.
Now nearly all head,

The rest of him—long feathery legs,
With feet that were nothing
But bunches of long hooks,
And wings that seemed almost too heavy to lift.
He had become an owl,

A sleepy owl, hated by men,
The bird with a screech you'd think a corpse
Might make if a corpse
Could float up from the underworld
With bad news for you and yours.

And maybe that spy got his deserts
For his mischief.
But what did the daughters of Achelous do wrong?
They too were turned into birds
In everything but their faces.

Was it bad luck by association
To have been Proserpina's playmates
At the flower-picking—
And did their singing, their miraculous chorus,
Fail to redeem them?

No, they too had gone searching for her
All over the world. In the end
They prayed for wings to cross the seas
And tell the ocean depths of their trouble.
The gods consented, and the amazed girls

Saw their bodies equipped with golden plumage,
And the wings and feet of birds. But their singing,
So loved by the gods, escaped this mutation.
Their tongues, their throats, their voices remained
        unaltered—
Live shrines of unearthly human voices.

Now Jupiter intervened
Between his brother and his grieving sister.
He parted the year's round into two halves.
From this day, Proserpina,
The goddess who shares both kingdoms, divides her
    year

Between her husband in hell, among spectres,
And her mother on earth, among flowers.
Her nature, too, is divided. One moment
Gloomy as hell's king, but the next
Bright as the sun's mass, bursting from clouds.

Arethusa

Ceres, happy again to have her daughter,
Returned to Arethusa, curious
To learn why she ran from home, and just how
She became a sacred fountain.

The pool grew calm as the goddess
Rose out of the depth.
She gathered up her green hair and from it
Wringing the heavy water began
The old story of how she was loved by a river.

"I was a nymph of Achaia.
None loved the woods,
And setting their hunting nets, as keenly as I did.
I was all action and energy,
And never thought of my looks.
Even so, my looks, yes, my beauty
Made others think of me.
The fame of my appearance burdened me.
The attractions
That all the other girls were sick to have
Sickened me, that I had them.
Because they attracted men, I thought them evil.

"There came a day
I had exhausted myself
In the Stymphalian Forest. The heat was frightening.

And my efforts, harrying the game,
Had doubled its effect on me.
I found a stream, deep but not too deep,
Quiet and clear—so clear,
Every grain of sand seemed magnified.
And so quiet, the broad clarity
Hardly dimpled.
The poplars and willows that drank at it
Were doubled in a flawless mirror.
I waded in—footsoles, ankles, knees.
Then stripped,
Hung my clothes on a willow
And plunged.
As I played there, churning the surface,
To and fro, diving to the bottom,
Swimming on my back, my side, my belly,
I felt a strange stir bulge in the current—
It scared me so badly
I scrambled up onto the bank.
A voice came after me:
'Why leave in such a hurry, Arethusa?'
It was Alpheus, in the swirl of his waters.
'Why leave in such a hurry?' he cried again.
I saw my clothes on the willow across the river.
I had come out on the wrong bank.
Naked as I was, I just ran—
That brought him after me
All the more eagerly—my nakedness
Though it was no invitation
Gave his assault no option.
I was like the dove in a panic
Dodging through trees when the hawk
Rides its slipstream
Tight as a magnet.

"The peak of Orchomenus went past,
And Psophis—
They were stepping stones
That my feet barely touched. Then Cyllene
And the knapped, flinty ridges
Of Maenalus, Erymanthus, and Elis—
The map rolled under me
As in a flight in a dream. He could not
Overtake me
But he could outlast me.
Over savannahs, mountains black with forest,
Pathless crags and gorges. But soon
The sun pressed on my back and I saw
That I ran in a long and leaping shadow—
The very shape of my terror—
And I heard the stones flying
From his striding feet, and his panting breath
That seemed to tug at my hair.

"In an agony of effort
I called to Diana:
'Help, or it's all over with me.
Remember how I carried your bow,
Your quiverful of arrows. Help me,
Help me, oh, help me.'

"The goddess heard and was stirred.
She brought up a dense mist
And hid me.
I smothered my gasping lungs. I tried
To muffle my heartbeat. And I froze.
I could hear the river-god, Alpheus,
Blindly casting about—
Twice he almost trod on me
Where I crouched under deep weeds.
'Arethusa!' he kept shouting. 'Arethusa!'

As if I would answer!
You can imagine what I was feeling—
What the lamb feels when the wolf's jaws
Are ripping the edge of the shed door.
Or what the hare feels
Peering through the wall of grass blades
When the circling hounds lift their noses.
But Alpheus persisted.
Circling the clump of mist, he could see clearly
My track that had gone in had not come out.
When I understood this
A sudden sweat chilled my whole body.
It streamed from me.
It welled from my hair. It puddled under my feet.
In the time it takes to tell you this
I had become a spring, a brisk stream,
A river, flowing away down the hillside.
But the river-god recognised me.
And he too dissolved his human shape,
Poured himself into his true nature
And mingled his current with my current.

"But Diana helped me again. She split earth open.
I dived into the gorge
And underground I came to Ortygia—
This land,
Which bears the name of my own beloved goddess,
Brought me back to light. That is my story."

Tiresias

One time, Jupiter, happy to be idle,
Swept the cosmic mystery aside
And draining another goblet of ambrosia
Teased Juno, who drowsed in bliss beside him:
"This love of male and female's a strange business.
Fifty-fifty investment in the madness,
Yet she ends up with nine-tenths of the pleasure."

Juno's answer was: "A man might think so.
It needs more than a mushroom in your cup
To wake a wisdom that can fathom which
Enjoys the deeper pleasure, man or woman.
It needs the solid knowledge of a soul
Who having lived and loved in woman's body
Has also lived and loved in the body of a man."

Jupiter laughed aloud: "We have the answer.
There is a fellow called Tiresias.
Strolling to watch the birds and hear the bees
He came across two serpents copulating.
He took the opportunity to kill
Both with a single blow, but merely hurt them—
And found himself transformed into a woman.

"After the seventh year of womanhood,
Strolling to ponder on what women ponder
She saw in that same place the same two serpents

Knotted as before in copulation.
'If your pain can still change your attacker
Just as you once changed me, then change me back.'
She hit the couple with a handy stick,

"And there he stood as male as any man."
"He'll explain," cried Juno, "why you are
Slave to your irresistible addiction
While the poor nymphs you force to share it with you
Do all they can to shun it." Jupiter
Asked Tiresias: "In their act of love
Who takes the greater pleasure, man or woman?"

"Woman," replied Tiresias, "takes nine-tenths."
Juno was so angry—angrier
Than is easily understandable—
She struck Tiresias and blinded him.
"You've seen your last pretty snake, for ever."
But Jove consoled him: "That same blow," he said,
"Has opened your inner eye, like a nightscope. See:

"The secrets of the future—they are yours."

Echo and Narcissus

When the prophetic vision awoke
Behind the blind eyes of Tiresias
And stared into the future,

The first to test how deeply he saw
And how lucidly
Was Liriope, a swarthy nymph of the fountain.

She was swept off her feet by the river Cephisus
Who rolled her into the bed of a dark pool,
Then cast her up on the shingle pregnant.

The boy she bore, even in his cradle,
Had a beauty that broke hearts.
She named this child Narcissus. Gossips

Came to Tiresias: "Can her boy live long
With such perfect beauty?" The seer replied:
"Yes, unless he learns to know himself."

All regarded these words as a riddle—
Till time solved them with a peculiar madness.
A stranger death completed the explanation.

In his sixteenth year Narcissus,
Still a slender boy but already a man,
Infatuated many. His beauty had flowered,

But something glassy about it, a pride,
Kept all his admirers at a distance.
None dared be familiar, let alone touch him.

A day came, out on the mountain
Narcissus was driving and netting and killing the deer
When Echo saw him.

Echo who cannot be silent
When another speaks. Echo who cannot
Speak at all
Unless another has spoken.
Echo who always answers back.

In those days, this nymph was more than a voice.
She had a pretty body.
But her prattle was the same—
Never anything more
Than the last word or two, the tail end
Of what she heard uttered by others,
Which she repeated over and over.

Juno had stricken her
With this odd affliction.
When Juno, following a tip-off,
Would be stalking Jupiter, to catch him
In some dell, with a nymph,
Echo made it her duty
To engage the goddess in an unending
Rigmarole of chatter. Till the nymph
Had given the god enough
To be let go.
Echo did this so often,
And so artfully, Juno
In a rage turned on her: "Your tongue
Has led me in such circles,
Henceforth

It will have to trail
Helplessly after others, uttering
Only the last words, helplessly,
Of what you heard last."

The moment Echo saw Narcissus
She was in love. She followed him
Like a starving wolf
Following a stag too strong to be tackled.
And like a cat in winter at a fire
She could not edge close enough
To what singed her, and would burn her.
She almost burst
With longing to call out to him and somehow
Let him know what she felt.
But she had to wait
For some other to speak
So she could snatch their last words
With whatever sense they might lend her.

It so happened, Narcissus
Had strayed apart
From his companions.
He hallooed them: "Where are you?
I'm here." And Echo
Caught at the syllables as if they were precious:
"I'm here," she cried, "I'm here" and "I'm here" and
    "I'm here."

Narcissus looked around wildly.
"I'll stay here," he shouted.
"You come to me." And "Come to me,"
Shouted Echo. "Come to me,
To me, to me, to me."
Narcissus stood baffled,
Whether to stay or go. He began to run,

Calling as he ran: "Stay there." But Echo
Cried back, weeping to utter it, "Stay there,
Stay there, stay there, stay there."
Narcissus stopped and listened. Then, more quietly,
"Let's meet halfway. Come." And Echo
Eagerly repeated it: "Come."

But when she emerged from the undergrowth
Her expression pleading,
Her arms raised to embrace him,
Narcissus turned and ran.
"No," he cried, "no, I would sooner be dead
Than let you touch me." Echo collapsed in sobs,
As her voice lurched among the mountains:
"Touch me, touch me, touch me, touch me."

Echo moped under the leaves.
Humiliated, she hid
In the deep woods. From that day
Like a hurt lynx, for her
Any cave was a good home.
But love was fixed in her body
Like a barbed arrow. There it festered
With his rejection. Sleeplessly
She brooded over the pain,
Wasting away as she suffered,
The petal of her beauty
Fading and shrivelling, falling from her—
Leaving her voice and bones.
Her bones, they say, turned
Into stone, sinking into the humus.
Her voice roamed off by itself,
Unseen in the forest, unseen
On the empty mountainside—
Though all could hear it
Living the only life left to Echo.

Narcissus had rebuffed her adoration
As he had the passionate attentions
Of many another nymph of the wilderness
And many another man.
One of these, mocked and rejected,
Lifted his hands to heaven:
"Let Narcissus love and suffer
As he has made us suffer.
Let him, like us, love and know it is hopeless.
And let him, like Echo, perish of anguish."
Nemesis, the corrector,
Heard this prayer and granted it.

There was a pool of perfect water.
No shepherd had ever driven sheep
To trample the margins. No cattle
Had slobbered their muzzles in it
And befouled it. No wild beast
Had ever dashed through it.
No bird had ever paddled there preening and bathing.
Only surrounding grasses drank its moisture
And though the arching trees kept it cool
No twigs rotted in it, and no leaves.

Weary with hunting and the hot sun
Narcissus found this pool.
Gratefully he stretched out full length,
To cup his hands in the clear cold
And to drink. But as he drank
A strange new thirst, a craving, unfamiliar,
Entered his body with the water,
And entered his eyes
With the reflection in the limpid mirror.
He could not believe the beauty
Of those eyes that gazed into his own.
As the taste of water flooded him

[*Echo and Narcissus*

So did love. So he lay, mistaking
That picture of himself on the meniscus
For the stranger who could make him happy.

He lay, like a fallen garden statue,
Gaze fixed on his image in the water,
Comparing it to Bacchus or Apollo,
Falling deeper and deeper in love
With what so many had loved so hopelessly.
Not recognising himself
He wanted only himself. He had chosen
From all the faces he had ever seen
Only his own. He was himself
The torturer who now began his torture.

He plunged his arms deep to embrace
One who vanished in agitated water.
Again and again he kissed
The lips that seemed to be rising to kiss his
But dissolved, as he touched them,
Into a soft splash and a shiver of ripples.
How could he clasp and caress his own reflection?
And still he could not comprehend
What the deception was, what the delusion.
He simply became more excited by it.
Poor misguided boy! Why clutch so vainly
At such a brittle figment? What you hope
To lay hold of has no existence.
Look away and what you love is nowhere.
This is your own shadow.
It comes with you. While you stay it stays.
So it will go
When you go—if ever you can go.

He could not go.
He wanted neither to eat nor to sleep.

Only to lie there—eyes insatiably
Gazing into the eyes that were no eyes.
This is how his own eyes destroyed him.

He sat up, and lifting his arms
Called to the forest: "You trees,
Was there ever a love
As cruel as mine is to me?
You aged voyeurs, you eavesdroppers,
Among all the lovers who have hidden
Under your listening leaves
Was there ever a love
As futureless as mine?
What I love is untouchable.
We are kept apart
Neither by seas nor by mountains
Nor by the locked-up gates of cities.
Nothing at all comes between us—
Only the skin of water.
He wants my love as I want his.
As I lean to kiss him
He lifts up his face to kiss me—
Why can't I reach him? Why can't he reach me?
In that very touch of the kiss
We vanish from each other—he vanishes
Into the skin of water.

"Who are you? Come out. Come up
Onto the land. I never saw beauty
To compare with yours. Oh, why do you always
Dodge away at the last moment
And leave me with my arms full of nothing
But water and the memory of an image?
It cannot be my ugliness
Or my age that repels you,
If all the nymphs are so crazy about me.

Your face is full of love
As your eyes look into my eyes.
I see it, and my hope shakes me.
I stretch my arms to you, you stretch yours
As eagerly to me. You laugh when I laugh.
I have watched your tears through my tears.
When I tell you my love I see your lips
Seeming to tell me yours—though I cannot hear it.

"You are me. Now I see that.
I see through my own reflection.
But it is too late.
I am in love with myself.
I torture myself. What am I doing—
Loving or being loved?
What can my courtship gain?
What I want, I am.
But being all that I long for—
That is my destitution.
Why can't I get apart from my body?
This is a new kind of lover's prayer.
To wish himself apart from the one he loves.

"This impotent grief
Is taking my strength
And my life.
My beauty is in full bloom—
But I am a cut flower.
Let death come quickly—
Carry me off
Where this pain
Can never follow.
The one I loved should be let live—
He should live on after me, blameless.
But when I go—both of us go."

Then Narcissus wept into the pool.
His tears shattered the still shrine
And his image blurred.
He cried after it: "Don't leave me.
If I cannot touch you at least let me see you.
Let me nourish my starving, luckless love—
If only by looking."
Then he ripped off his shirt,
And beat his bare chest with white fists.
The skin flushed under the blows.
When Narcissus saw this
In the image returned to perfection
Where the pool had calmed—
It was too much for him.
Like wax near the flame,
Or like hoar-frost
Where the first ray of the morning sun
Creeps across it,
He melted—consumed
By his love.
Like Echo's the petal of his beauty
Faded, shrivelled, fell—
He disappeared from his own eyes.
Till nothing remained of the body
That had driven Echo to distraction.

Echo was watching all this misery.
Remembering how it happened before
To her, when he ran from her,
Her anger blazed
But her pity smothered it.
And when he moaned, "Alas," she wept,
And groaned. "Alas." His last words,
As he gazed into the dark pool,
"Farewell, you incomparable boy,
I have loved you in vain"

Returned from her lips with sorrow doubled:
"I have loved you in vain."
And after his last "Farewell"
Came her last "Farewell."
He pillowed his head on the grass.
So finally death
Closed the eyes that had loved themselves too much.

When he entered the Land of the Dead
Narcissus could not resist it—
He ran straight to the banks of the Styx
And gazed down at the smear of his shadow
Trembling on the fearful current.
His sisters, the nymphs of the fountains,
Cropped their hair and mourned him
In a lamenting song—and far off,
Wandering heartbroken among the hills
Echo sang the refrain.

When men came with timber
To build a pyre, and with crackling torches
For the solemnity
That would reduce Narcissus
To a handful of dust in an urn—
No corpse could be found.
But there, in the pressed grass where he had perished,
A tall flower stood unbroken—
Bowed, a ruff of white petals
Round a dainty bugle centre
Yellow as egg yolk.

Yes, it was this quiet woodland flower
Trumpeted the fame of Tiresias
Throughout Achaia.

Erysichthon

Some are transformed just once
And live their whole lives after in that shape.
Others have a facility
For changing themselves as they please.

Proteus, who haunts the shadowy seas
That scarf this earth, is glimpsed as a young man
Who becomes of a sudden a lion
That becomes a wild boar ripping the ground,

Yet flows forward, hidden, through grass, without
    sound
As a serpent, that emerges
As a towering bull under down-bent horns,
Or hides, among stones, a simple stone.

Or stands as a tree alone.
Or liquefies, and collapses, shapeless,
Into water, a pouring river. Sometimes
He is the river's opposite—fire.

Another with a similar power
Was Erysichthon's daughter,
The wife of Autolycus. Her father
Gave to the gods nothing but mockery.

Without a qualm he cut down every tree
In the sacred grove of Ceres—
An ancient wood that had never, before that day,
Jumped to the axe's stroke.

Among those trees
One prodigious oak was all to itself
A tangled forest. Its boughs were bedecked with
    wreaths
And votive tributes—each for a prayer

Ceres had sometime granted. Dryads there
Danced a holy circle around its bole
Or joined hands to embrace it—
A circumference of twenty paces.

Erysichthon ignores all this as
He assesses the volume of its timber,
Then orders his men to fell it.
Seeing their reluctance, he roars:

"If this tree were your deity, that every clown adores,
And not merely a tree you think she favours,
Nevertheless, those twigs away there at the top
Would have to come down now, as the rest falls."

He snatches an axe—and hauls
The weight of the broad head up and back.
But in that moment, as the blade hangs
Poised for the first downstroke, shudderings

Swarm through the whole tree, to its outermost twigs
And a groan bursts from the deep grain.
At the same time
Every bough goes grey—every leaf

Whitens, and every acorn whitens.
Then the blade bites and the blood leaps
As from the neck of a great bull when it drops
Under the axe at the altar.

Everybody stares paralysed.
Only one man protests. The Thessalian
Erysichthon turns with eyes stretched
Incredulous. "Your pious cares," he bellows,

"Are misplaced." And he follows
That first swing at the oak with another
At the protester's neck, whose head
Spins through the air and bounces.

Then the oak, as he turns back to it, pronounces,
In a clear voice, these words:
"I live in this tree. I am a nymph,
Beloved by Ceres, the goddess.

"With my last breath, I curse you. As this oak
Falls on the earth, your punishment
Will come down on you with all its weight.
That is my consolation. And your fate."

Erysichthon ignored her. He just kept going,
Undercutting the huge trunk, till ropes
Brought the whole mass down, jolting the earth,
Devastating the underbrush around it.

All the nymphs of the sacred grove mourned it.
Dressed in black, they came to Ceres,
Crying for the criminal to be punished,
Bewailing the desecration. The goddess listened.

Then the summer farms, the orchards, the vineyards,
The whole flushed, ripening harvest, shivered
As she pondered how to make his death
A parable of her anger.

If his cruelty, greed, arrogance
Had left him a single drop of human feeling
What the goddess did now
Would have drained mankind of its pity.

She condemned him
To Hunger—
But infinite, insatiable Hunger,
The agony of Hunger as a frenzy.

Destiny has separated Hunger
So far from the goddess of abundance
They can never meet; therefore Ceres
Commissioned a mountain spirit, an oread:

"Hear what I say and do not be afraid.
Far away to the north of Scythia
Lies a barren country, leafless, dreadful:
Ice permanent as iron, air that aches.

"A howling land of rocks, gales and snow.
There mad Hunger staggers. Go. Bid Hunger
Take possession of Erysichthon's belly.
Tell her she has power over all my powers

"To nourish Erysichthon. Let all I pour
Or push down this fool's gullet only deepen
His emptiness. Go. My dragon-drawn chariot
Will make the terrific journey seem slight."

The nymph climbed away and her first halt
Was the top of Caucasus.
She soon found Hunger raking with her nails
To bare the root of a tiny rock-wort

Till her teeth could catch and tear it.
In shape and colour her face was a skull, blueish.
Her lips a stretched hole of frayed leather
Over bleeding teeth. Her skin

So glossy and so thin
You could see the internal organs through it.
Her pelvic bone was like a bare bone.
The stump wings of her hip bones splayed open.

As she bowed, her rib-cage swung from her backbone
In a varnish of tissue. Her ankle joints
And her knee joints were huge bulbs, ponderous,
        grotesque,
On her spindly shanks. The oread

Knew danger when she saw it. She proclaimed
The command of the goddess from a safe distance.
The whole speech only took a minute or so—
Yet a swoon of hunger left her trembling.

She got away fast.
All the way back to Thessaly
She gave the dragons their head.
Now hear me.

Though Hunger lives only in opposition
To Ceres, yet she obeys her. She soars through
        darkness
Across the earth, to the house of Erysichthon
And bends above the pillow where his face

Snores with open mouth.
Her skeletal embrace goes around him.
Her shrunk mouth clamps over his mouth
And she breathes

Into every channel of his body
A hurricane of starvation.
The job done, she vanishes,
She hurtles away, out of the lands of plenty,

As if sucked back
Into the vacuum—
Deprivation's hollow territories
That belong to her, and that she belongs to.

Erysichthon snores on—
But in spite of the god of sleep's efforts
To comfort him, he dreams he sits at a banquet
Where the food tastes of nothing. A nightmare.

He grinds his molars on air, with a dry creaking,
Dreaming that he grinds between his molars
A feast of nothing, food that is like air.
At last he writhes awake in convulsive

Cramps of hunger. His jaws
Seem to have their own life, snapping at air
With uncontrollable eagerness to be biting
Into food and swallowing—like a cat

Staring at a bird out of reach.
His stomach feels like a fist
Gripping and wringing out
The mere idea of food.

He calls for food. Everything edible
Out of the sea and earth. When it comes
Dearth is all he sees where tables bend
Under the spilling plenty. Emptying

Bowls of heaped food, all he craves for
Is bigger bowls heaped higher. Food
For a whole city cannot sate him. Food
For a whole nation leaves him faint with hunger.

As every river on earth
Pours its wealth towards ocean
That is always sweeping for more,
Draining the continents,

And as fire grows hungrier
The more fuel it finds,
So, famished by food,
The gullet of Erysichthon, gulping down

Whatever its diameter can manage
Through every waking moment,
Spares a mouthful
Only to shout for more.

This voracity, this bottomless belly,
As if his throat opened
Into the void of stars,
Engulfed his entire wealth.

His every possession was converted
To what he could devour
Till nothing remained except a daughter.
This only child deserved a better father.

His last chattel, he cashed her in for food.
He sold her, at the market.
But she was far too spirited
To stay as a bought slave.

Stretching her arms towards the sea, she cried:
"You who ravished my maidenhead, save me."
Neptune knew the voice of his pretty victim
And granted the prayer. Her new owner,

Who minutes ago was admiring the girl he had
    bought,
Now saw only Neptune's art—featured
And clothed like a fisherman. Perplexed,
He spoke to this stranger directly.

"You with your fishing tackle, hiding your barbs
In tiny gobbets of bait—may you have good weather
And plenty of silly fish that never notice
The hook till it's caught them!—can you tell me

"Where is the girl who was here a moment ago?
Her hair loose, and dressed in the cheapest things,
She was standing right here where her footprints—
Look—stop, and go no further. Where is she?"

The girl guessed what the god had done for her.
She smiled to hear herself asked where she might be.
Then to the man parted from his money:
"I'm sorry, my attention has been fixed

"On the fish in this hole. But I promise you,
By all the help I pray for from Neptune,
Nobody has come along this beach
For quite a while—and certainly no woman."

The buyer had to believe her. He went off, baffled.
The girl took one step and was back
In her own shape. Next thing,
She was telling her father. And he,

Elated, saw business. After that
On every market he sold her in some new shape.
A trader bought a horse,
Paid for it and found the halter empty

Where a girl sat selling mushrooms.
A costly parrot escaped its purchaser
Into an orchard—where a girl picked figs.
One bought an ox that vanished from its pasture

Where a girl gathered cowslips.
So Erysichthon's daughter plied her talent
For taking any shape to cheat a buyer—
Straight and crooked alike.

All to feed the famine in her father.
But none of it was enough. Whatever he ate
Maddened and tormented that hunger
To angrier, uglier life. The life

Of a monster no longer a man. And so,
At last, the inevitable.
He began to savage his own limbs.
And there, at a final feast, devoured himself.

Semele

Juno was incensed when she learned it:
Jove had impregnated Semele.
Curses
Came bursting out of her throat, but she swallowed
    them
Hissing: "Anger is lost on Jupiter. Only

"Let me get my hands on that woman.
As sure as I am Juno, the Queen of Heaven,
As sure as I grasp the sceptre
And am Jove's wife and sister,
As sure as I am at very least his sister,

"I shall destroy that whore.
Let others excuse her. They say she takes nothing
If this taste of his love is all she takes.
They say she's no more trespassed on my marriage
Than a cloud-shadow crossing a mountain.

"They should know the fact.
His brat is in her womb.
And that is a kind of marriage—
Durable as the life of that creature.
Jupiter's own child—out of her womb!

"More than I ever gave him.
A splendid-looking woman—

And so pleased with herself, to be so splendid.
Her pleasure is a delusion.
Her beauty comes at a cost, she will find.

"I am not the daughter of Saturn
If she does not stumble very soon
Headlong into hell's horrible river,
Pushed there and shoved under
By the loving caresses of none other

"Than her darling, the high god Jupiter."
Juno rose from her throne
Like a puff of smoke from a volcano.
In a globe of whirling light
She arrived at the home of Semele.

Semele
Looked up at a shadow. There,
Standing on her threshold, a gummy old woman—
White wisps,
A sack of shrivelled skin propped on a stick,

Bent as if broken-backed,
Tottering at each step to stay on her feet,
And her voice
Quavering like a dying pulse. This figure
Was the very double of Beroe—

Semele's old nurse from Epidaurus.
Semele recognised and welcomed
Her old nurse. She never doubted a moment.
Their gossiping began to circle,
Touching at Semele's swollen belly.

Juno sighed. Her lizard throat trembled.
"Ah, I pray you are right.

I pray that Jupiter is the sire, as you say.
But who can be sure?
Something about it smells fishy to me.

"You wouldn't be the first simple virgin
To hear an unscrupulous seducer
Reveal his greatest secret—that he is a god.
Even if he spoke the truth and you are right—
Even if the babe in your womb is Jove's—

"Supposition will not satisfy
The questions
That will surely occur to the coming child.
That child
Is going to demand real proof.

"Jupiter should give you real proof
That he is himself. Ask him to face you
Naked as for Juno in heaven,
In all his omnipotence and glory,
The great god of the triple-headed sceptre."

Listening to the twisty words of Juno
Semele heard
Only the purest wisdom.
She asked her divine lover for a love-gift—
A gift she would name only if it were granted.

Jupiter smiled: "Whatever you want—name it,
You shall have it. I swear
On the terror who holds all heaven in awe,
The god of hell's river, you shall have it."
Semele's laugh was as triumphant

As she was ignorant
Of the game she was playing.

She laughed
To have won the simple trick
That would wipe her out of existence

So easily. "I want to see you," she said,
"Exactly as Juno sees you when she opens
Her arms and body to you. As if I were Juno,
Come to me naked—in your divine form."
Too late

Jove guessed what she was asking.
He tried to gag her
With his hand but her tongue
And her lips had hurried it all out
And he had heard it. He groaned.

His oath could no more be retracted
Than her words could be unuttered.
Yes, God wept a little
Gathering the foggy clouds around him
As he withdrew into heaven.

Now he piled above him the purple
Topheavy thunderheads
Churning with tornadoes
And inescapable bolts of lightning.
Yet he did what he could to insulate

And filter
The nuclear blast
Of his naked impact—
Such as had demolished Typhoeus
And scattered his hundred hands.

He chose
A slighter manifestation

[*Semele*

Fashioned, like the great bolts, by the Cyclops
But more versatile—known in heaven
As the general deterrent.

Arrayed in this fashion
Jove came to the house of Cadmus' daughter.
He entered her bedchamber,
But as he bent over her sleeping face
To kiss her

Her eyes opened wide, saw him
And burst into flame.
Then her whole body lit up
With the glare
That explodes the lamp—

In that splinter of a second,
Before her blazing shape
Became a silhouette of sooty ashes
The foetus was snatched from her womb.
If this is a true story

That babe was then inserted surgically
Into a makeshift uterus, in Jove's thigh,
To be born, at full term, not from his mother
But from his father—reborn. Son of the Father.
And this was the twice-born god—the god Bacchus.

Peleus and Thetis

Proteus, old as the ocean,
Said to Thetis: "Goddess
Of all the salt waters,
When you bear a son the boy will be
The wonder of the world.
He will make a man of himself
So far superior to his father
His father's fame will be—to have been his father."
Jupiter heard the prophecy just in time
To deflect his lust
From the maidenhead of Thetis.
He switched it
To the next on his list. But as a precaution,
Too well aware of his own frailty,
He sent a substitute to neutralise
The prize of the prediction and its sequel:
Peleus, his grandson, son of Aeacus.
"Go," he commanded. "No matter what it takes
To bring it about, impregnate that virgin."

Tucked into Haemonia's coast is a bay
Between promontories, deep incurved,
Like a sickle.
A perfect harbour if only the water were deeper.
But the sea sweeps in
Barely covering a plain of pale sand.
The beach is perfect,

No seaweed, and the sand
Powdery light, yet firm to the foot.
The hanging bulge of the land is plumped with
    myrtles.
Beneath those leaves a cave climbs from the sea.
It looks like the work of man. But a deity used it.
This was the secret bedchamber of Thetis.
Naked, she surfed in on a dolphin
To sleep there. And there Peleus found her.

He woke her with a kiss.
First she was astonished, then furious.
He applied all his cunning to seduce her.
He exhausted his resources. None of it worked.
His every soft word hardened her colder.
If they had been two cats, he was thinking,
She would have been flattened to the wall,
Her mask fixed in a snarl, spitting at him.
He took his cue from that. Where argument
Fails, violence follows. His strength
Could have trussed her up like a chicken
If she had stayed the woman he woke with a kiss.
But before he knew
He was grappling with an enormous sea-bird,
Its body powerful as a seal, and its beak
Spiking his skull like a claw-hammer.
A bird that was suddenly a wren
Escaping towards the tangle of myrtles,
Bolting past his cheek like a shuttlecock
That he caught with a snatch of pure luck,
And found himself
Gripping a tigress by the shag of her throat
As her paw hit him with the impact
Of a fifty-kilo lump of snaggy bronze
Dropped from a battlement.

He rolled from the cave and landed flat on his back
In cushioning shallow water.

Then he slaughtered sheep,
Burned their entrails, heaped incense
Onto the fatty blaze, poured wine
Into the salt wash and called on the sea-gods,
Till a shade, from the depth-gloom beyond,
Darkened into the bay's lit shallows,
And a voice hissed from the tongues of suds
That shot up the sand: "Son of Aeacus,
This woman can be yours if you can catch her
Sleeping as before in her cavern.
But this time, bind her, bind her tight with thongs,
Before she wakes. Then hang on to her body
No matter what it becomes, no matter what monster.
Do not let her scare you—
However she transforms herself, it is her,
Dodging from shape to shape, through a hundred
        shapes.
Hang on
Till her counterfeit selves are all used up,
And she reappears as Thetis."
This was the voice of Proteus. It ceased
And the long shape faded from the shallows.

Peleus hid in the myrtles. Towards sundown
The goddess came up from the deep water,
Rode into the bay, climbed into her cave
And stretched out on her couch.

She was hardly asleep
When the noosed thongs jerked tight.
Her ankles and her wrists made one bunch.
Her feet and hands were a single squirming cluster,

As if she were to be carried, slung from a pole,
Like an animal.

Peleus clinched his knot, then bundled her up
In his arms, and embraced her with all his might
As her shapes began to fight for her.
He shut his eyes and hung on, ignoring
Her frenzy of transformations
Till they shuddered to stillness. She knew she was
    beaten
By that relentless grip. "Heaven has helped you,"
She panted. "Only heaven
Could have given me to you, and made me yours."

Then he undid her bonds. As he massaged
The circulation into her hands and feet
His caresses included her whole body.
She was content to let them take possession
Of her skin, her heart, and, at last, of her womb
Where now he planted Achilles.

Actaeon

Destiny, not guilt, was enough
For Actaeon. It is no crime
To lose your way in a dark wood.

It happened on a mountain where hunters
Had slaughtered so many animals
The slopes were patched red with the butchering
    places.

When shadows were shortest and the sun's heat
    hardest
Young Actaeon called a halt:
"We have killed more than enough for the day.

"Our nets are stiff with blood,
Our spears are caked, and our knives
Are clogged in their sheaths with the blood of a
    glorious hunt.

"Let's be up again in the grey dawn—
Back to the game afresh. This noon heat
Has baked the stones too hot for a human foot."

All concurred. And the hunt was over for the day.
A deep cleft at the bottom of the mountain
Dark with matted pine and spiky cypress

Was known as Gargaphie, sacred to Diana,
Goddess of the hunt.
In the depths of this goyle was the mouth of a cavern

That might have been carved out with deliberate art
From the soft volcanic rock.
It half-hid a broad pool, perpetually shaken

By a waterfall inside the mountain,
Noisy but hidden. Often to that grotto,
Aching and burning from her hunting,

Diana came
To cool the naked beauty she hid from the world.
All her nymphs would attend her.

One held her javelin,
Her quiverful of arrows and her unstrung bow.
Another folded her cape.

Two others took off her sandals, while Crocale
The daughter of Ismenus
Whose hands were the most artful, combing out

The goddess' long hair, that the hunt had tangled,
Bunched it into a thick knot,
Though her own hair stayed as the hunt had
        scattered it.

Five others, Nephele, Hyale, Phiale
Psecas and Rhanis, filled great jars with water
And sluiced it over Diana's head and shoulders.

The goddess was there, in her secret pool,
Naked and bowed
Under those cascades from the mouths of jars

In the fastness of Gargaphie, when Actaeon,
Making a beeline home from the hunt
Stumbled on this gorge. Surprised to find it,

He pushed into it, apprehensive, but
Steered by a pitiless fate—whose nudgings he felt
Only as surges of curiosity.

So he came to the clearing. And saw ripples
Flocking across the pool out of the cavern.
He edged into the cavern, under ferns

That dripped with spray. He peered
Into the gloom to see the waterfall—
But what he saw were nymphs, their wild faces

Screaming at him in a commotion of water.
And as his eyes adjusted, he saw they were naked,
Beating their breasts as they screamed at him.

And he saw they were crowding together
To hide something from him. He stared harder.
Those nymphs could not conceal Diana's whiteness,

The tallest barely reached her navel. Actaeon
Stared at the goddess, who stared at him.
She twisted her breasts away, showing him her back.

Glaring at him over her shoulder
She blushed like a dawn cloud
In that twilit grotto of winking reflections,

And raged for a weapon—for her arrows
To drive through his body.
No weapon was to hand—only water.

So she scooped up a handful and dashed it
Into his astonished eyes, as she shouted:
"Now, if you can, tell how you saw me naked."

That was all she said, but as she said it
Out of his forehead burst a rack of antlers.
His neck lengthened, narrowed, and his ears

Folded to whiskery points, his hands were hooves,
His arms long slender legs. His hunter's tunic
Slid from his dappled hide. With all this

The goddess
Poured a shocking stream of panic terror
Through his heart like blood. Actaeon

Bounded out across the cave's pool
In plunging leaps, amazed at his own lightness.
And there

Clear in the bulging mirror of his bow-wave
He glimpsed his antlered head,
And cried: "What has happened to me?"

No words came. No sound came but a groan.
His only voice was a groan.
Human tears shone on his stag's face

From the grief of a mind that was still human.
He veered first this way, then that.
Should he run away home to the royal palace?

Or hide in the forest? The thought of the first
Dizzied him with shame. The thought of the second
Flurried him with terrors.

But then, as he circled, his own hounds found him.
The first to give tongue were Melampus
And the deep-thinking Ichnobates.

Melampus a Spartan, Ichnobates a Cretan.
The whole pack piled in after.
It was like a squall crossing a forest.

Dorceus, Pamphagus and Oribasus—
Pure Arcadians. Nebrophonus,
Strong as a wild boar, Theras, as fierce.

And Laelaps never far from them. Pterelas
Swiftest in the pack, and Agre
The keenest nose. And Hylaeus

Still lame from the rip of a boar's tusk.
Nape whose mother was a wolf, and Poemenis—
Pure sheep-dog. Harpyia with her grown pups,

Who still would never leave her.
The lanky hound Ladon, from Sicyon,
With Tigris, Dromas, Canace, Sticte and Alce,

And Asbolus, all black, and all-white Leuca.
Lacon was there, with shoulders like a lion.
Aello, who could outrun wolves, and Thous,

Lycise, at her best in a tight corner,
Her brother Cyprius, and black Harpalus
With a white star on his forehead.

Lachne, like a shaggy bear-cub. Melaneus
And the Spartan-Cretan crossbreeds
Lebros and Agriodus. Hylactor,

With the high, cracked voice, and a host of others,
Too many to name. The strung-out pack,
Locked onto their quarry,

Flowed across the landscape, over crags,
Over cliffs where no man could have followed,
Through places that seemed impossible.

Where Actaeon had so often strained
Every hound to catch and kill the quarry,
Now he strained to shake the same hounds off—

His own hounds. He tried to cry out:
"I am Actaeon—remember your master,"
But his tongue lolled wordless, while the air

Belaboured his ears with hounds' voices.
Suddenly three hounds appeared, ahead,
Raving towards him. They had been last in the pack.

But they had thought it out
And made a short cut over a mountain.
As Actaeon turned, Melanchaetes

The ringleader of this breakaway trio
Grabbed a rear ankle
In the trap of his jaws. Then the others,

Theridamus and Oristrophus, left and right,
Caught a foreleg each, and he fell.
These three pinned their master, as the pack

Poured onto him like an avalanche.
Every hound filled its jaws
Till there was hardly a mouth not gagged and
    crammed

With hair and muscle. Then began the tugging and the
    ripping.
Actaeon's groan was neither human
Nor the natural sound of a stag.

Now the hills he had played on so happily
Toyed with the echoes of his death-noises.
His head and antlers reared from the heaving pile.

And swayed—like the signalling arm
Of somebody drowning in surf.
But his friends, who had followed the pack

To this unexpected kill,
Urged them to finish the work. Meanwhile they shouted
For Actaeon—over and over for Actaeon

To hurry and witness this last kill of the day—
And such a magnificent beast—
As if he were absent. He heard his name

And wished he were as far off as they thought him.
He wished he were among them
Not suffering this death but observing

The terrible method
Of his murderers, as they knotted
Muscles and ferocity to dismember

Their own master.
Only when Actaeon's life
Had been torn from his bones, to the last mouthful,

Only then
Did the remorseless anger of Diana,
Goddess of the arrow, find peace.

Myrrha

Cinyras, the son of Paphos,
Might well have been known as Fortune's darling
If only he'd stayed childless.

The story I am now going to tell you
Is so horrible
That fathers with daughters, wherever you are,
Had better not listen to it—
I beg you to stay clear.
Or if you find my song irresistible
Let your ear
Now become incredulous.
May you convince yourselves this never happened.

Or if you find yourselves
Believing this crime and horrified by it—
You must, above all, believe
In the punishment, the awesome punishment,
The gods allotted to it.

If nature can let any person fall
Into crimes as vile as this
I congratulate our corner of the world—
So lucky to lie so far
From the soil
That nursed this enormity.

Let Panchaia be praised for its balsam,
Zedoary, cinnamon, and for the teeming
Variety of its herbs, and for its abundance
Of trees bearing incense—
But while myrrh grows there it cannot be envied.

The cost of that bush was too great.
Whatever arrow pierced the heart of Myrrha
Cupid absolutely disowns it.
Whatever torches kindled the flames in her body
He denies they were his.

One of hell's three horrible sisters
Brought a firebrand from the flickering tarpit
And an armful of serpents
Anointed with their own venom
And took possession of her.

Hatred for one's father is a crime.
Myrrha's love for her father
Was a crime infinitely worse.

The court of King Cinyras hummed with suitors.
From every degree of the compass they had come,
The princes of the East—
Haughty rivals for the King's daughter
Who wanted nothing to do with any of them.
Choose, Myrrha, before the story twists,
Choose from all these men in your father's palace—
Excluding only one.

Myrrha felt the stirring secret
Serpent of her craving and the horror
That came with it.
"What is happening to me?" she whispered.

"What am I planning?"
She prayed to the gods: "You watchers in heaven,
Help me to strangle this.
I pray
By the sacred bond between child and parent
Let me be spared this.
Do not permit this criminal desire
To carry me off—if it is criminal.
Is it criminal?
Is it unnatural?
For all the creatures it is natural—
When the bull mounts the heifer, his daughter,
Neither feels shame.
A stallion fights to breed from his own daughter.
A billy goat will impregnate his daughter
As soon as any other little nanny.
And the birds—the birds—
No delicate distinctions deter them.
All mate where they can.
How lucky they are, those innocents,
Living within such liberties.
Man has distorted that licence—
Man has made new laws from his jealousy
To deprive nature of its nature,
Yet I have heard that nations exist
Who make a virtue of just this—fathers
Marry their daughters, mothers marry their sons—
To keep the blood in the family,
And give to both daughters and sons
Possession of their deepest happiness—
The bliss of their infancy as a wedding present.

"But I was born here, not there.
Born into the prison of this palace,
A prisoner of these laws. What am I doing?
Thoughts are running away with me.

I must not let such hopes roam so freely.
And yet, by every contract and custom,
Cinyras owns my love.
It would be a crime indeed to withhold it.
And if it were not for one small accident—
That he begat me—
I could give him my love, as his bride.

"But—because I am his—he can never be mine.
How if I were a stranger?
I should get away,
Get out of this land—but could I ever
Get out of my guilt? Out of my love?
My evil obsession keeps me here
Where I can be near him,
Look at him, speak to him, touch him, kiss him,
Though that is the limit of it.
Wretch, what more can you hope for?
Do you want to lie netted
In a mesh of family conundrums—
Sister to your son,
Co-wife to your mother, your brother's mother?
Remember the Furies,
The snake-haired, dreadful sisters
Who climb from the hell of conscience
Whirling their torches.
Be careful. While you are still guiltless,
Before you have set a foot wrong,
Do not so much as think of taking
The first step. Mighty Nature
Set this prohibition
Between a human father and his daughter.
Fear it.
I know what you want. It is because
You are who you are that you cannot have it.
Cinyras is noble. He lives by law.

And yet what if he fell
Into just such agonies of love—"

Meanwhile
Cinyras was wholly preoccupied
By the superfluity of suitors.
He saw only one solution.
He cited their names and lands and possessions
To his daughter—
Then simply asked her to choose.

Long minutes
Myrrha stood staring at her father.
For her, nothing else existed.
Her brain stormed—but to no purpose,
While her eyes brimmed as if they melted.
Cinyras pitied his child.
What he saw was modesty tormented.
He dried her face and kissed her.
He told her not to cry—while she clung
To his neck, half swooning at his kisses.
And when he asked her just what kind of husband
She wanted, she whispered: "One like you."
Cinyras understood nothing. He laughed:
"My darling, never let anything change your devotion
To me." When she heard that word "devotion"
Her heart broke up in her body. She stood there
Like a beast at the altar, head hanging.

Midnight. Mankind sprawled
In sleep without a care.
But Myrrha writhed in her sheets.
To cool the fiery gnawings throughout her body
She drew deep gasping breaths.
They made the flames worse.
Half of her prayed wildly—

In despair under the crushing
Impossibility—and half of her coolly
Plotted how to put it to the test.
She was both aghast at her own passion
And reckless to satisfy it.

Like a great tree that sways,
All but cut through by the axe,
Uncertain which way to fall,
Waiting for the axe's deciding blow,
Myrrha,
Bewildered by the opposite onslaughts
Of her lust and her conscience,
Swayed, and waited to fall.
Either way, she saw only death.
Her lust, consummated, had to be death;
Denied, had to be death.

With a huge effort
She got up out of bed,
Tied her girdle to a door lintel
And made a noose.
"Cinyras," she sobbed. "O my darling,
When you see this, please understand it."
She pushed her numb, drained face
Through the noose. But as she drew the knot
Tight to the nape of her neck
She fainted. The lintel jerked at her weight.

Her old nurse, who lay in the next room,
Slept lightly as a sparrow.
She found herself listening
To the girl's despairing soliloquy.
Instantly she was up and through the door.
She shrieked at the suicide.
She tugged the knot loose.

She tore her own garments, and beat at her breasts,
She laid the limp girl on the floor—

Then she wept—
Embraced the girl and wept
And asked her why she should want to do such a
    thing.
Myrrha had recovered. She lay silent.
She simply lay there
Letting her worst moment do its worst.
Too slow to end it all
And then being caught in the act
Seemed to leave her now with less than nothing.

But the old nurse was persistent.
She clawed down her white hairs,
She bared the shrivelled skins of her breasts
And begged the girl, by this ruin
Of the cradle of her first years,
To tell her the secret.

Myrrha moaned and twisted from the questions.

The nurse came in closer, determined
To get at the truth. And she promised
Not only to keep her secret:
"I may be old," she said,
"But that may make it easier for me to help you.
If some lunatic fit has fallen on you
From some power in the air,
From something you have eaten, some place you have
    sat in,
I know who can cure it.
If somebody has bewitched you, I know
The rituals to unwind the spell and bind it
Round the witch's neck.

Or if you have unsettled the gods
I know which offerings can appease them.
What else can it be?
Your home and future are secure.
Your father and mother are happy, they reign in their
    prime."

As if she had heard nothing else
That single word "father" went through Myrrha
Like a hot iron, and she sighed in misery.
The nurse missed that clue. But she guessed
Love was at the bottom of it.
So she dug away stubbornly
Embracing and straining the girl's ripeness
To her own withered rack.
"I know," she whispered at last, "I know your
    sickness.
You are in love.
And I am the very one who can best help you.
Not a breath of this shall come to your father."

Again at the word "father"
Myrrha choked a cry.
"Go away," she wailed. She wrenched herself
From the nurse's clasp
And pitched onto her bed,
Burying her face in pillows.
"Leave me alone," she sobbed.
"Don't take the last rag of my self-respect."

And when the nurse persisted: "Stop. Don't ask.
What you are wanting to know is pure evil."
The old woman recoiled.
And now it was fear, not age, that made her tremble.

But more determined than ever
She clutched Myrrha's feet in her old fingers
Threatening to tell her father everything
About that noose
Unless she shared her secret. At the same time
She promised perfect loyalty
If she would confide it—
Yes, and her help. She promised her help.

Myrrha looked up and flung her arms
Around her old nurse. Her tears
Splashed down the scraggy breasts.
Now she tried to confess. But every effort
Was stifled as she hid her face again
And gagged herself with her robe.
At last she managed: "My mother is so lucky
To have such a man for her husband—"
Then her voice was overwhelmed
By the flood of sobs that came with it.

But the nurse had heard enough.
Now she knew she had the truth
As her white hair bushed out
In a halo of horror
And she felt her body go cold.
Her slow words of caution, of wisdom,
Dragging up
From some rarely used depth,
Began to admonish Myrrha.
As if mere words could have a hope
Of altering such a passion.
Myrrha shook them off
As she shook the tears from her eyes.

She knew
The nurse's words were all true.

But her passion was deaf
As well as blind.
And if it could not satisfy itself
No matter what it destroyed in the act
It was happy to die that very moment.

"This is great folly," the nurse said then.
"Death is never an option, only an error.
Myrrha, you shall have—" Here she paused.
Her tongue shied from the words "your father."
"You shall have—I promise it, I call
Heaven to witness, you shall have your will."

Now came the festival of Ceres.
Married women, robed in laundered whiteness,
Brought the goddess the first-fruits
Of the harvest. For these women
Through nine days and nights
Love or the slightest contact with a man
Was forbidden.

Cenchreis, the wife of Cinyras,
The mother Myrrha so painfully envied,
Was one of the celebrants
Wrapped in the white gown of the mysteries.
Nine days and nine nights
The King's bed was to be empty.

That first evening Cinyras, drowsily
Sipping a last glass, found himself
Listening to the nurse's strange news—
About an incredibly beautiful girl
Madly in love with him.
Idly, he asked the girl's age,
And the nurse said, "Same as Myrrha."

"Bring her tonight," said the King, with hardly a
    thought.

The nurse returned to Myrrha, jubilant—
"Success," she hissed. "Success."
It was then, as that sharp word "success"
Went past her ear
That Myrrha felt a premonitory shiver,
The quick touch of a shadow of terror.
Then she let her joy lift her off her feet.

The moon had gone down,
Clouds covered the stars,
When Myrrha, like a wide-eyed sleepwalker,
Hypnotised by a dream of wild lust
Stepped from her chamber—
The heavens above gave her no light.
Icarus had covered his face
And Erigone, lifted to heaven by pure love of her
    father,
Hid her eyes.

Three times
Myrrha stumbled
As if her very feet rebuked her.
Three times
A screech owl, death's *doppelgänger*,
The bird with the sewn-up face,
Saluted her evil fate
With its rasping laugh.
But she ignored all omens,
Finding refuge from her shame
In the pitch darkness, that hid her almost from herself.

Her left hand
Clung to the hand of her old nurse.

Her right hand
Groped for invisible obstacles
As if she were blind.
The old woman went swiftly.
She knew the map of the palace with her eyes closed.

And here
Was the door of the King's bedroom.
The door swung wide.
Suddenly Myrrha was standing
In the dark chamber
Where the King breathed.

Her legs almost went from beneath her.
The blood drained from her face and head—
Unrecognised, she knew
She still had time to get out.

But more and more horrified by herself,
More and more sick with guilt,
She let the old nurse
Lead her toward the bed where the King waited.

"She is yours,"
Was all the old woman whispered.
Gently she pushed Myrrha forward
Till she felt that reluctant, trembling body
Lifted weightless from her
Into the dark tent of the bed.

Then she crabbed away in the dark
Fleeing the disaster she had created
And that had already forgotten her.

The father
Welcomed his own flesh and blood

Into the luxury
Of the royal bed.
He comforted her,
Mistaking her whimpering struggle of lust and
      conscience
For girlish panic.
It could be
To soothe her he called her "my child"
Or even "my daughter"
And maybe when she called him "father"
He supposed that made her first yielding
Somehow easier for her—
So the real crime, that the King thought no crime,
Let nothing of its wickedness be omitted.

After her father had crammed her with his seed
Myrrha left him
Finding her way now without difficulty—
Her womb satisfied
With its prize:
A child conceived in evil.

The next night father and daughter did it again
In the pitch darkness.
The same, night after night. On the ninth night
Cinyras made a mistake.
He let curiosity take over.
He prepared a lamp. That he lit
And held high, as she lay there,
Revealing the form and the face
Of his bedmate—
His daughter.

Now all the guilt was his.
Too huge and elemental
For words

His anguish
Was a roar throughout the palace.
He snatched his sword from its scabbard.
But Myrrha dived from his chamber
Into the night, dodging like a bat,
And escaped him.

She went on,
Crossed her father's kingdom,
Forsook Panchaia,
Left Arabia's palms far behind her.

Till a nine-month meandering journey
Brought her to Sabaea.
There she rested the kicking freight
That she could carry no further,
Utterly disgusted with her life
But afraid of dying.
She had no idea what to pray for,
So prayed without thinking:

"O you gods,
If there are any gods with patience enough
To listen to me
Who deserve
The most pitiless judgement
Which I would welcome—
I only fear that by dying
I would pollute the dead,
Just as my life contaminates the living.
Give me some third way, neither wholly dead
Nor painfully alive. Remove me
From life and from death
Into some nerveless limbo."

Venus and Adonis
(and Atalanta)

A power in the air hears the last prayer
Of the desperate. Myrrha's prayer to be no part
Of either her life or her death was heard and was
     answered.

The earth gripped both her ankles as she prayed.
Roots forced from beneath her toenails, they burrowed
Among deep stones to the bedrock. She swayed,

Living statuary on a tree's foundations.
In that moment, her bones became grained wood,
Their marrow pith,

Her blood sap, her arms boughs, her fingers twigs,
Her skin rough bark. And already
The gnarling crust has coffined her swollen womb.

It swarms over her breasts. It warps upwards
Reaching for her eyes as she bows
Eagerly into it, hurrying the burial

Of her face and her hair under thick-webbed bark.
Now all her feeling has gone into wood, with her
     body.
Yet she weeps,

The warm drops ooze from her rind.
These tears are still treasured.
To this day they are known by her name—Myrrh.

Meanwhile the meaty fruit her father implanted
Has ripened in the bole. Past its term,
It heaves to rive a way out of its mother.

But Myrrha's cramps are clamped in the heart-wood's
    vice.
Her gagged convulsions cannot leak a murmur.
She cannot cry to heaven for Lucina.

Nevertheless a mother's agony
Strained in the creaking tree and her tears drench it.
For pity, heaven's midwife, Lucina,

Lays her hands on the boughs in their torment
As she recites the necessary magic.
The trunk erupts, the bark splits, and there tumbles

Out into the world with a shattering yell
The baby Adonis. Nymphs of the flowing waters
Cradle him in grasses. They wash him

With his mother's tears. Bittermost envy
Could only glorify such a creature.
A painter's naked Cupid to perfection—

The god's portrait without his arrow quiver
Or his bow. Here, subtlest of things,
Too swift for the human eye, time slips past.

And this miraculous baby of his sister,
Sired by his grandpa, just now born of a bush,
Barely a boy, in the blink of an eye is a man

        [*Venus and Adonis*

Suddenly more beautiful than ever—
So beautiful the great Venus herself,
Hovering over the wonder, feels awe.

Then the boy's mother, pent by Venus
In that shrub of shame, finds her revenge.
The goddess falls helplessly for Adonis.

Venus plucking kisses from her Cupid
Snagged her nipple on an unnoticed arrow
Sticking from his quiver. She pushed him away—

But was wounded far worse than she feared.
Pierced by the mortal beauty of Adonis
She has forgotten Cythera's flowery island,

Forgotten the bright beaches of Paphos,
Forgotten Cnidos, delicate as its fish,
Amathus, veined with costly metals. Neglected

Even Olympus. She abstains from heaven
Besotted by the body of Adonis.
Wherever he goes, clinging to him she goes.

She who had loved equally the shade
And her indolence in it, who had laboured
Only as a lily of the valley,

Now goes bounding over the stark ridges,
Skirts tucked high like the huntress, or she plunges
Down through brambly goyles, bawling at hounds,

Hunting the harmless; the hare who sees best
        backwards,
Hinds with painful eyes like ballerinas,
Tall stags on their dignity. She has nothing

To do with fatal boars. She shuns wolves,
Their back teeth always aching to crack big bones.
Bears with a swipe like a dungfork. Lions,

Lank bellies everlastingly empty,
That lob over high bomas, as if weightless,
With bullocks in their jaws. "These," she cried,

"O my beloved, are your malefic planets.
Never hesitate to crush a coward
But, challenged by the brave, conceal your courage.

"Leave being bold, my love, to the uglier beasts.
Else you stake my heart in a fool's gamble.
Let Nature's heavier criminals doze on

"Or you may win your glory at my cost.
The beauty, the youth, the charms that humbled
        Venus,
Feel silly and go blank when suddenly a lion

"Looks their way. They have no influence
On whatever lifts a boar's bristles,
Or on the interests or on the affections

"Of any of that gang. The tusk of the boar
Is the lightning jag that delivers the bolt.
The ignorant impact of solidified

"Hunger in the arrival of a lion
Turns everything to dust. I abhor them!"

"But why should you abhor them?"

                              "There is a lesson
These coarse brutes can teach us. But first,

This hunters' toil is more than my limbs are used to.
Look, that kindly poplar has made cool

"A bed of shade in the grass, just for us."
So Venus pillowed her head on the chest of Adonis.
Then, to her soft accompaniment of kisses:

"Once the greatest runner was a woman—so swift
She outran every man.
It is true. She could and she did.
But none could say which was more wonderful—
The swiftness of her feet or her beauty.

"When this woman questioned the oracle
About her future husband
The god said: 'Atalanta,
Stay clear of a husband.
Marriage is not for you. Nevertheless

" 'You are fated to marry.
And therefore fated, sooner or later, to live
Yourself but other.' The poor girl,
Pondering this riddle, alarmed,
Alerted, alone in a thick wood,

"Stayed unmarried.
The suitors who kept at her stubbornly
She met
With a fearful deterrent:
'You can win me,' she told them,

" 'Only if you can outrun me.
That is to say, if you will race against me.
Whoever wins that race—he is my husband.
Whoever loses it—has lost his life.
This is the rule for all who dare court me.'

"Truly she had no pity.
But the very ferocity
Of this grim condition of hers
Only lent her beauty headier power—
Only made her suitors giddier.

"Hippomenes watched the race.
'What fool,' he laughed, 'would wager life itself
Simply to win a woman—
With a foregone conclusion against him?
This is a scheme to rid the world of idiots.'

"But even as he spoke he saw the face
Of Atalanta. Then as her dress opened
And fell to her feet
He saw her dazzling body suddenly bared.
A beauty, O Adonis, resembling mine

"Or as yours would be if you were a woman.

"Hippomenes' brain seemed to turn over. His
        arms,
As if grabbing to save himself as he slipped,
Were reaching towards her, fingers hooked,
And he heard his own voice
Coming like somebody else's: 'What am I saying?

" 'I did not know, I never guessed
What a trophy
You run for—'
And there, as he stammered and stared,
His own heart was lost.

"Suddenly he was terrified of a winner.
He prayed that all would fail and be executed.

'But why,' he muttered, 'am I not out among
        them
Taking my chance?
Heaven helps those who give it something to
        help.'

"These words were still whirling in his head
As her legs blurred past him.
Though her velocity was an arrow
As from a Turkish bow of horn and sinew
The shock-wave was her beauty.

"Her running redoubled her beauty.
The ribbon-ties at her ankles
Were the wing-tips of swallows.
The ribbon-ties at her knees
Were the wing-tips of swifts.

"Her hair blazed above her oiled shoulders.
And the flush on her slender body
Was ivory tinted
By rays that glow
Through a crimson curtain.

"And while this hero gazed with drying mouth
It was over.
Atalanta stood adjusting her victor's chaplet
And her defeated suitors, under the knife,
Sprawled as they coughed up her bloody
        winnings.

"Hippomenes ignored the draining corpses.
He stepped forward—his eyes gripping hers.
'Why do you scry for fame, Atalanta,
In the entrails
Of such pathetic weaklings?

" 'Why not run against me?
If I win
You will not be shamed—only surpassed
By the son of Megareus,
Who was sired by Neptune, god of the sea.

" 'I am Hippomenes—
A grandson of the god of the oceans.
I have not disappointed expectations.
If my luck fails, by the fame of Hippomenes
Your fame shall be that much more resplendent.'

"Atalanta was astonished as she felt
Her heart falter. Her legs began to tremble.
Her wild rage to conquer seemed to have kneeled
In a prayer to be conquered.
She murmured:

" 'Which god, jealous of beautiful youth,
Plots now to slay this one?
Putting it into his head to fling away life.
As I am the judge:
Atalanta is not worth it.

" 'It is not his beauty that makes me afraid
Though it well might.
It is his innocence, his boyishness
Touches me, and hurts me.
He is hardly a boy. He is a child.

" 'Yet with perfect courage,
Contemptuous of death.
Also fourth in descent, as he claims, from the sea-
        god.
Also he loves me
And is ready to die if he cannot have me.

" 'Listen, stranger,
Get as far away from me as you can
By the shortest route.
Marriage with me is death.
Go while you can move.

" 'My bridal bed, my virgin bed, is a sump
Under the executioner's block.
Go and go quickly.
No other woman will refuse you.
The wisest will do all she can to win you.

" 'Yet why should I bother myself?
After so gladly killing so many
Why should I care now? Die if you must.
If these poor corpses here cannot deter you,
If you are so sick of your life—then die.

" 'They will say: because he dared to love her
She killed him. I shall have to hear:
Her thanks for his fearless love was a shameful
        death.
This will bring me fame—but ill-fame.
Yet none of it is my fault.

" 'You cannot win, Hippomenes,
Forget me.
If only your insanity could shrink
Into your feet as a superhuman swiftness!
Look at him. His face is like a girl's.

" 'In me there sleeps evil for both of us.
Do not wake it up. Go quietly away.
You belong to life. But believe me,
If Fate had not made my favour lethal
You alone would be my choice.'

"Atalanta knew nothing about love
So she failed
To recognise love's inebriation
As it borrowed her tongue to pronounce these
    words.
She was hardly aware of what they meant.

"But her father, and the crowd, demanded the
    race.
And Hippomenes was already praying: 'O Venus,
You gave me this great love—now let me keep it.'
A quirk of air brought his prayer to my hearing.
Moved, I moved quickly.

"The most precious acre in Cyprus
Is my temple's orchard. A tree grows there
Of solid gold. With leaves of green gold
On boughs of white gold. Among those leaves
Hang apples of red gold. I picked three.

"Visible only to Hippomenes
I taught him the use of these apples.
Then at a blast from the trumpets
Both shot from their marks.
Their feet flickered away and the dust hung.

"They could have been half-flying over water
Just marring the shine.
Or over the silky nape of a field of barley.
Hippomenes felt the crowd's roar lifting him on:
'Hippomenes! You can win! Hippomenes!'

"And maybe Atalanta
Was happier than he was to hear that shout
As she leaned back on her hips, reining back
The terrible bolt of speed in her dainty body,

And clung to him with her glance even as she left
    him

"Tottering as if to a halt, labouring for air
That scorched his mouth and torched his lungs,
With most of the course to go. This was the
    moment
For flinging one of my apples out past her—
He bounced it in front of her feet and away to
    the left.

"Startled to see such a gorgeous trinket
Simply tossed aside, she could not resist it.
While she veered to snatch it up
Hippomenes was ahead, breasting the crest
Of the crowd's roar.

"But Atalanta came back in with a vengeance.
She passed him so lightly he felt to be stumbling.
Out went the second apple.
As if this were as easy she swirled and caught it
Out of a cloud of dust and again came past him.

"Now he could see the flutter of the crowd at the
    finish.
'O Venus,' he sobbed, 'let me have the whole of
    your gift!'
Then with all his might he hurled
The last apple
Past and beyond her—into a gulley

"Choked with tumbled rock and thorn. She
    glimpsed it
Vanishing into a waste
Of obstacles and lost seconds.

With two gold apples heavier at each stride
And the finish so near, she tried to ignore it.

"But I forced her to follow. And the moment she
    found it
That third apple I made even heavier.
Lugging her three gold prizes far behind
Her race was lost. Atalanta belonged to the
    winner.
So their story begins.

"But tell me, Adonis, should he have given me thanks
And burned costly perfumes in my honour?
Neither thanks nor perfumes arrived. He forgot my
    help.

"Anger overtook me. I was hurt.
I swore I would never again be slighted so.
My revenge would scare mankind for ever.

"Now hear the end of the story. This fine pair
Worn out with their wanderings, in a deep wood
Found a temple
Built long since for Cybele, Mother of the Gods,
Whose face is a black meteorite.

"Both thought they were tired enough that night
To sleep on the stone paving. Till I kissed
The ear of Hippomenes
With a whisper. As my lips touched him he
    shivered
Into a fit of lust like epilepsy.

"Under the temple was a cave shrine
Hollowed in solid bedrock and far older

Than the human race. An unlit crypt.
It was walled
With wooden images of the ancient gods.

"This was the sanctum doomed Hippomenes
Now defiled,
Sating himself on the body of Atalanta.
The desecrated wooden images
Averted their carved faces in horror.

"And the tower-crowned Mother of All, Cybele,
Considered plunging both
As they copulated
Into Styx, the tarpit of bubbling hell.
But that seemed insufficient to her.

"Instead she dropped maned hides
Over their sweating backs. Hardened and hooked
Their clutching fingers into talons. Let
Their panting chest-keels deepen. Let them sweep
The dust with long tails. Gargoyle-faced,

"And now with speech to match, these godless
      lovers
Rumble snarls, or cough, or grunt, or roar.
They have the thorny scrub for a nuptial chamber
And are lions—their loathsome fangs obedient
Only to the bridle-bits of Cybele.

"O dear love,
These and the others like them, that disdain
To give your hounds a run but come out looking
      for the hunter,
For my sake, O dear boy, let them lie.
Do not ruin our love with your recklessness."

Her lesson done, the goddess climbed with her swans
Towards lit clouds. Meanwhile, as Adonis
Pondered her parable to find a meaning,

His hounds woke a wild boar in a wallow.
When this thug burst out, his boar-spear's point
Glanced off the bone into the hump of muscle.

The boar deftly hooked the futile weapon
Out of the wound and turned on the hunter,
Overtook the boy's panic scramble,

Bedded its dagger tusks in under his crotch
Then ploughed him with all its strength as if
        unearthing
A tough tree's roots, till it hurled him aside, emptied.

Venus, afloat on swansdown in the high blue,
Still far short of Paphos, felt the shock-wave
Of the death-agony of Adonis.

She banked and diving steeply down through cirrus
Sighted her darling boy where he sprawled
Wallowing in a mire of gluey scarlet.

She leapt to the earth, ripping her garment open.
She clawed her hair and gouged her breasts with her
        nails,
Pressing her wounds to his wounds as she clasped him

And screaming at the Fates: "You hags shall not
Have it all your way. O Adonis,
Your monument shall stand as long as the sun.

"The circling year itself shall be your mourner.
Your blood shall bloom immortal in a flower.
Persephone preserved a girl's life

"And fragrance in pale mint. I shall not do less."
Into the broken Adonis she now dripped nectar.
His blood began to seethe—as bubbles thickly

Bulge out of hot mud. Within the hour
Where he had lain a flower stood—bright-blooded
As those beads packed in the hard rind

Of a pomegranate. This flower's life is brief.
Its petals cling so weakly, so ready to fall
Under the first light wind that kisses it,

We call it "windflower."

Pygmalion

If you could ask the region of Amathus
Where the mines are so rich
Whether it had wanted those women
The Propoetides,
You would be laughed at, as if you had asked
Whether it had wanted those men
Whose horned heads earned them the name Cerastae.

An altar to Zeus,
God of hospitality, stood at the doors
Of the Cerastae, soaked—
A stranger would assume—with the blood
Of the humbly sacrificed
Suckling calves and new lambs of Amathus.
Wrong. They butchered their guests.

Venus was so revolted to see offered
Such desecrated fare
She vowed to desert Ophiusa
And her favoured cities.
But she paused: "The cities," she reasoned,
"And the places I love—
What crime have these innocents committed?

"Why should I punish all
For a few? Let me pick out the guilty
And banish or kill them—

Or sentence them to some fate not quite either
But a dire part of both.
The fate for such, I think, is to become
Some vile thing not themselves."

The horns of the Cerastae suggested
One quick solution for all—
Those men became bullocks. As for the others,
The Propoetides—
Fools who denied Venus divinity—
She stripped off their good names
And their undergarments, and made them whores.

As those women hardened,
Dulled by shame, delighting to make oaths
Before the gods in heaven
Of their every lie, their features hardened
Like their hearts. Soon they shrank
To the split-off, heartless, treacherous hardness
Of sharp shards of flint.

The spectacle of these cursed women sent
Pygmalion the sculptor slightly mad.
He adored woman, but he saw
The wickedness of these particular women
Transform, as by some occult connection,
Every woman's uterus to a spider.
Her face, voice, gestures, hair became its web.
Her perfume was a floating horror. Her glance
Left a spider-bite. He couldn't control it.

So he lived
In the solitary confinement
Of a phobia,
Shunning living women, wifeless.

Yet he still dreamed of woman.
He dreamed
Unbrokenly awake as asleep
The perfect body of a perfect woman—
Though this dream
Was not so much the dream of a perfect woman
As a spectre, sick of unbeing,
That had taken possession of his body
To find herself a life.

She moved into his hands,
She took possession of his fingers
And began to sculpt a perfect woman.
So he watched his hands shaping a woman
As if he were still asleep. Until
Life-size, ivory, as if alive
Her perfect figure lay in his studio.

So he had made a woman
Lovelier than any living woman.
And when he gazed at her
As if coming awake he fell in love.

His own art amazed him, she was so real.
She might have moved, he thought,
Only her modesty
Her sole garment—invisible,
Woven from the fabric of his dream—
Held her as if slightly ashamed
Of stepping into life.

Then his love
For this woman so palpably a woman
Became his life.

Incessantly now
He caressed her,
Searching for the warmth of living flesh,
His finger-tip whorls filtering out
Every feel of mere ivory.

He kissed her, closing his eyes
To divine an answering kiss of life
In her perfect lips.
And he would not believe
They were after all only ivory.

He spoke to her, he stroked her
Lightly to feel her living aura
Soft as down over her whiteness.
His fingers gripped her hard
To feel flesh yield under the pressure
That half wanted to bruise her
Into a proof of life, and half did not
Want to hurt or mar or least of all
Find her the solid ivory he had made her.

He flattered her.
He brought her love-gifts, knick-knacks,
Speckled shells, gem pebbles,
Little rainbow birds in pretty cages,
Flowers, pendants, drops of amber.
He dressed her
In the fashion of the moment,
Set costly rings on her cold fingers,
Hung pearls in her ears, coiled ropes of pearl
To drape her ivory breasts.

Did any of all this add to her beauty?
He gazed at her adorned, and his head ached.
But then he stripped everything off her

And his brain swam, his eyes
Dazzled to contemplate
The greater beauty of her beauty naked.

He laid her on his couch,
Bedded her in pillows
And soft sumptuous weaves of Tyrian purple
As if she might delight in the luxury.
Then, lying beside her, he embraced her
And whispered in her ear every endearment.

The day came
For the festival of Venus—an uproar
Of processions through all Cyprus.
Snowy heifers, horns gilded, kneeled
Under the axe, at the altars.

Pygmalion had completed his offerings.
And now he prayed, watching the smoke
Of the incense hump shapelessly upwards.
He hardly dared to think
What he truly wanted
As he formed the words: "O Venus,
You gods have power
To give whatever you please. O Venus,
Send me a wife. And let her resemble—"
He was afraid
To ask for his ivory woman's very self—
"Let her resemble
The woman I have carved in ivory."

Venus was listening
To a million murmurs over the whole island.
She swirled in the uplift of incense
Like a great fish suddenly bulging
Into a tide-freshened pool.

She heard every word
Pygmalion had not dared to pronounce.

She came near. She poised above him—
And the altar fires drank her assent
Like a richer fuel.
They flared up, three times,
Tossing horns of flame.

Pygmalion hurried away home
To his ivory obsession. He burst in,
Fevered with deprivation,
Fell on her, embraced her, and kissed her
Like one collapsing in a desert
To drink at a dribble from a rock.

But his hand sprang off her breast
As if stung.
He lowered it again, incredulous
At the softness, the warmth
Under his fingers. Warm
And soft as warm soft wax—
But alive
With the elastic of life.

He knew
Giddy as he was with longing and prayers
This must be hallucination.
He jerked himself back to his senses
And prodded the ivory. He squeezed it.
But it was no longer ivory.
Her pulse throbbed under his thumb.
Then Pygmalion's legs gave beneath him.
On his knees
He sobbed his thanks to Venus. And there
Pressed his lips

On lips that were alive.
She woke to his kisses and blushed
To find herself kissing
One who kissed her,
And opened her eyes for the first time
To the light and her lover together.

Venus blessed the wedding
That she had so artfully arranged.
And after nine moons Pygmalion's bride
Bore the child, Paphos,
Who gave his name to the whole island.

Hercules and Deianira

Hercules, the son of Jupiter,
Was bringing his new bride home
When he came to the river Evenus.

Burst banks, booming torrent
Where there had been a ford. Hercules
Had no fear for himself, only for his wife.

A centaur galloped up. This was Nessus
Familiar with the bed of that river.
Broad haunch, deep shoulder, powerful vehicle
For forcing a way through strong water.

"Let me take her over," he offered.
"Big as you are, Hercules,
You will be swept off your feet, but you can swim."

Thinking only of getting across
This earth-shaking menace
That stunned the air with mist,
The Boeotian hero hoisted his darling
Onto the centaur's back.

Deianira clung there, white with fear—
Paralysed
Between her dread of the river
And her dread of the goat-eyed centaur.

Who now plunged straight into
The high-riding boils of brown water.

Hercules wasted no time either.
He hurled his club and his heavy bow
Right across to the far bank, and muttered:
"No river resists me."
Then, without pausing
To seek some broader, quieter reach of water,
Leapt in as he was, at the narrowest place,
Dragging the drogue of his arrow quiver
And the ponderous pelt of the lion,
Breasting the race right there, where it tightened
In a blaze of brown foam through the narrows.

He came out hard-skinned and glistening
On the other side
And had just picked up his bow
When a human scream tossed clear
Of the river's rumbling stampede
And he saw Nessus
Galloping away with Deianira.

"You fool," roared Hercules,
"Do you think your horse hooves are equal
To your mad idea?
Do you think you can plant your family tree
Between me and mine?
Nessus, the cure for you is on its way.
Neither respect for me
Nor your father's howls in hell
Chained on his wheel of fire
Can deflect you from the forbidden woman.
But I shall overtake you,
Not on my feet, but flying
On the feather of a weapon."

As these words left the mouth of Hercules
His arrow arrived,
And Nessus was looking down
At the barbed head, raw with blood,
Jutting from his breastbone
Before he felt it splinter his vertebrae.

He wrenched the arrow clean through him
And the blood burst free,
Thudding jets, at front and back—
Blood already blackened
By the arrow's medication—
The lethal juices of the Lernaean Hydra.

This blood brought a last brain-wave to Nessus.
He saw its use. "Let me," he groaned,
"Leave an avenger behind me."
Then stripping off his shirt
And soaking it in the hot fountain
Pumping from his chest
Gave it to Deianira.
"With my dying words," he whispered,
"I give you this love-charm, to win man's love.
No man who wears it can resist it."

The years went by. The triumphs of Hercules
Grew familiar to the whole world
As did Juno's hatred of him.

—

His conquest of Oechalia,
That looked like just another, was his last.

Returning from this victory, intending
To offer up thanks to Jupiter

At Cenaeum, on flaming altars,
Hercules himself was overtaken
By a whisper,
By rumour—
Rumour who loves to spice big bowls of the false
With a pinch of the true,
And who, gulping her own confections,
Grows from nearly nothing to fill the whole world.
Rumour reached his wife well before him
And offered her something irresistible,
Telling her that her husband, the tower of man,
Had fallen for Iole. What you fear
Overtakes you. Deianira
Had always dreaded this moment.
Her screams had waited too long
For exactly this. After the screams
She fell to the ground sobbing.
But straightaway pulled herself together:
"Why wail—except to amuse my rival?
She'll be at the door any minute.
A plan! Cunning!
The brain—before it's too late!
Before he marries her.
Scold? Or be silent?
Go home to Calydon, and hide there
Under your father's throne?
Or sit it out here?
Disappear, and mystify both—
Or stay and poison their pleasures
With my noise and nuisance
If nothing else?
Or remind myself I am the sister
Of Meleager
And frighten the life out of everybody
With the way I kill her—
Illustrating my agony on her body,

Demonstrating, incidentally,
What it means to be jilted?"

As she revolved her options
She recalled the dying gaze of the centaur—
And his last breath—making sacred
The promise in the strawberry shirt of blood.
She saw her perfect solution.
Unknowing as she was
Of any hidden meaning in the garment
This unfortunate woman handed the shirt
That would complete her misery
To Hercules' factotum—one Lichas.

She called it a welcoming,
A homecoming gift, for her husband.

Unknowing as she sent it, the hero received it—
Put off his lion pelt
And pulled over his shoulders the bile
That made his arrows fatal—
Bile crushed from the gall
Of the Hydra so famously defeated.

He had lit the first altar flames
For the high god.
Now he sprinkled incense into the flames
Chanting his prayers of gratitude, and pouring
Wine from goblets over the altar marble.

But already the venom in the weave of his shirt,
Softened and activated
By the heat of the altar,
Was soaking into his skin.
It reached and touched his blood. Then of a sudden
Struck through his whole body.

Amazed at the flush of pain
But refusing to acknowledge it
Or that anything of the sort could be happening
To him
Hercules for a while
Did not even gasp.
He thought he had shrugged off worse.
Then came a bigger pang—
A prong of pure terror
That jabbed his very centre
And opened
A whole new order of agony.
At last he understood.
His roar shook the woods of Oeta.
His frantic hands knew they were too late
As he scattered the altar-stones and tore
At the folds of the horrible garment.
Wherever the weave came away
It lifted sheets of steaming skin with it.
Either it clung,
Stronger than he was, or tore free
Only where the muscles tore free,
Writhing rags and rope-ends of muscle,
Baring the blue shine of thick bones.

The blood in all his veins had become venom.
His body was one blaze,
As if steam exploded
Where a mass of white-hot iron
Plunged into ice.

All being was agony, bottomless.
His heart pounded flame.
His shape melted in bloody plasm.
His sinews cracked and shrank.
His bones began to char.

Clawing at the stars, he cried:
"O Juno, daughter of Saturn,
Are you gloating?
Lean out of heaven and smile
At what is happening to me.
Glut your depraved heart on this banquet.
Or if I am so pathetic
That even my destroyer, yes, even you
Have to pity me
Then let me be rid of my life.
You are my stepmother, give me a gift,
A fitting gift from you,
Give me this death quickly,
Remove this soul you hate so much
And torture so tirelessly,
This soul that has survived, in relentless toil,
For this finale.
Did I rid the earth of Busiris,
The king who draped his temples
With the blood of travellers?
Did I pluck Antaeus
From the nurse of his infinite strength—
The breasts of his mother Earth—
Denying him any refreshment there,
Till he perished?
Is this why I never hesitated
To embrace those three-bodied horrors,
The Spanish herdsman, and Cerberus,
The dog at the gate of hell?
Are these the hands
That twisted the head of the giant bull down
And pinned his horn in the earth?
The hands that helped Elis
And the waters of Stymphalus
And the woods of Parthenius—
The hands that brought me

The prize of the Amazons,
A sword-belt of worked gold—
The hands that picked the apples of Hesperus
From the coils of the unsleeping serpent?
I barely paused for the Arcadian boar.
The centaurs were helpless against me.
The multiplication of the Hydra's heads
Were profitless to the monster.
And the man-eating horses of Diomed,
Gorged on human flesh,
Grown homicidal on their diet—
Drinking human blood, stalled and bedded
On the rags of human corpses—
I saw them, I slaughtered them,
And threw their master's carcase on top of the heap.
The Nemean lion went limp
In the grip of these fingers.
I took revolving heaven on these shoulders.
I never wearied of the labours
You, Juno, forced me to undertake.
You ran out of commands
Before I grew tired of obeying them.
But this is one labour too many.
Fire is turning me into itself.
Courage and weapons are futile.
I have become a leaf in a burning forest.
While King Eurystheus, my enemy,
Eats and laughs and feels invigorated
Among all the others who trust in gods."

This was the speech
That burst from the bloody wreckage
Of the great warrior
As he careered over the hills of Oeta—
Like a wild bull
Dragging the barbed spear

That the hunter fixed in his vitals
Before he fled.

Some saw him
Tugging at the shirt's last tatters,
Now inextricably
The fibres of his own body,
Uprooting trees, belabouring the faces of cliffs,
Reaching for his father in heaven.

In the blur of this frenzy, Hercules
Saw the feet of Lichas
Sticking from a crevice.
He had crammed his head and body in there
With such desperate fear
He thought he was all hidden.
But Hercules' pain had become madness.
He screamed: "Lichas—you
Threw this net over me. You trapped me
In this instrument of torture.
You were great Juno's cat's-paw
To strip my skeleton."
And Lichas was jerking in air
Like a rabbit
Dragged out by the hind legs.
He babbled excuses and scrabbled
For Hercules' knees to embrace them—

Too late, Hercules' arm
Was already whirling like a sling,
And like a slingstone Lichas
Shot into the sky, a dwindling speck
Out over the Euboean Sea.
As he went he hardened to stone.
As rain, they say, in the freezing winds
Hardens to snow, and the spinning snow

Is packed into hard hailstones.
Terror, we're told, boiled off his body liquids,
Baking him to stone. So, petrified,
He began to fall.
A rock, he splashed
Into the sea, far out.
He is still there, a crag in the swell,
A man-shaped clinker of fear,
Feared by sailors, who shun it
As if it might be alive. They call it Lichas.

Now Hercules, most famous
Son of the high god,
Felled thick trees on the top of Oeta,
And built a pyre.
He summoned Philoctetes, son of Poeas,
And gave him his bow, his quiver
And the arrows
Destined to return to the city of Troy.

With the help of Philoctetes
He kindled the squared stack of tree trunks.
And draping over it
His robe—the skin of the Nemean lion—
He stretched himself full length on top of that,
Head pillowed on his club,
And as the flames took hold, and the smoke boiled up,
Gazed into space like a guest
Lolling among the wine-cups,
Head wreathed with festive garlands.

Now flames savaged the whole pile
With elemental power
Like a pride of squabbling lions,
Worrying at limbs that ignored them,
Engulfing a hero who smiled in contempt.

The gods watched, distraught
To see the champion of the earth
Disintegrating in a blue shimmer,
Till Jupiter consoled them.
"You are anxious for my son. That is good.
I am happy to rule
Over gods who feel gratitude
Towards one who helped them.
His exploits have earned your admiration.
Your admiration for him warms me too.
His honour is my honour.
But do not be perturbed by these flames
Where Oeta seems to erupt.
The fire can take pleasure in Hercules
Only through what he had from his mother.
What he had from me
Is incombustible, indestructible,
Eternal—
Immune to flame, intangible to death.
That part has completed its earthspan.
So now—I shall lift it into heaven
Knowing you will rejoice to welcome it.

"If there is one among you
Who resents
This deification of my son
They will have to swallow all ill-feeling
And agree
Hercules has earned his reward."

The gods approved. Even Juno
Heard her husband out with a calm gaze.
Only the slightest frown flicked her eyebrow
At the touch of that last sentence.

While Jupiter was speaking, the fire
Removed every trace of Hercules
That fire could get a grip on.
His mother's boy had vanished.
In his place glowed the huge cast
Of the child of Jove.
The snake sloughs its age and dullness
In a scurf of opaque tatters,
Emerging, new-made, in molten brilliance—
So the Tirynthian hero emerged
More glorious, greater, like a descended god.

Then his omnipotent father hoisted him
Through clouds, in a four-horse chariot,
And fixed him among the constellations, massive.
Atlas grunted under the new weight.

The Birth of Hercules

Old Alcmene of Argolis,
Hercules' mother, had Iole
To hear her incessant grieving remembrance

Of her son's triumphs—that the world had watched
In amazement. To her, his anxious mother,
Each new task had come as a fresh disaster.

At the end, Hercules had asked Hyllus
To take Iole in, to his hearth and heart.
Iole carried the hero's unborn child.

"O Iole," cried Alcmene, "when your time comes
And you call on Lucina to help you,
I pray you may find favour, as I did not.

"Lucina, she who eases the way for women
When they perform their miracle of labour,
For me did the opposite. Having to listen

"To Juno's command, not to my prayers,
She made my time almost fatal to me.
The sun had gone through nine signs, entering the
    tenth,

"And Hercules, created for travail,
Was so enormous in me, it was plain
Only Jove could have sired him.

"My cramps were soon beyond what can be borne.
Now as I think of it a deathly sweat
Chills me. The old terror snatches at me.

"Seven days and nights I lay screaming.
I clawed at the sky, begging Lucina
To help me with her attendants—the gods of birth.

"She came, but she came from Juno—
Already bribed by Juno, and happy,
To toss my life to Juno's malevolence.

"She listened to me as if I were her music,
Sitting alone by the altar, at the front door,
Her right leg over and twisted around her left.

"And her hands knitted together with locked fingers
Blocking my baby's birth.
As my pushing began, she muttered her magic,

"Trapping the babe in the tunnel.
I writhed, I was out of my mind with pain.
I cursed Jupiter for his unconcern.

"None of it was any good.
My cries would have softened flint.
I begged to be let die.

"The women of Thebes, who were with me,
Amplified my cries, my prayers, my pleading,
Trying to comfort me. It was all useless.

"But I had a servant there, a quick-witted girl,
Galanthis—the most beautiful hair, red-gold—
Low-born, but dear to me for her loyalty.

"She recognised Juno's mischief.
And running in and out with cloths and water,
Noticed Lucina, sitting contorted at the altar,

"And in mid-stride cried: 'Good news.
Whoever you are, now is your lucky chance
To congratulate a fortunate woman.

" 'Alcmene of Argolis is thanking the gods!
At last—her beautiful child is beautifully born.'
Lucina leaped to her feet in dismay

"Freeing her tangled limbs and braided fingers
And as Lucina's body undid its knot
My child slid out, effortless, into the world.

"They say Galanthis laughed at Lucina—
Openly, to have fooled her so completely.
But as she laughed the angered goddess caught her

"By that hair, and dragged her to the ground full
            length,
And held her there, however she fought to get up,
And there transformed her forearms into short legs,

"And changed her whole body, and, letting her hair
Keep its colour and cover her, released her
A bounding and spitting weasel. A weasel!

"And since a lie issuing between her lips
Had helped a woman deliver her baby,
The weasel delivers her offspring through her mouth.

"But she is brisk and tireless as ever
And as before is here, there, everywhere,
All over my house."

The Death of Cygnus

Under Troy's wall, in mid-battle,
Cygnus, the son of Neptune,
Had gone through the Greeks twice
And sent a freshly butchered thousand
Tumbling into the underworld. Opposite—
The chariot of Achilles, through the Trojans,
A tornado through a dense forest,
Had left a swath of shattered trunks,
Vital roots in the air, a tangle of limbs.
Achilles was looking for Hector.
But Hector's humiliation
Had been deferred a decade into the future.
Meanwhile, here stood Cygnus,
With arrogant scowl and blood-washed weapons,
The champion of the moment. Achilles
Fixed his attention on him.
"Think yourself lucky," he shouted,
"As you leave your pretty armour to me,
That it was Achilles who killed you."
Then he drove his team straight at him,
And sent a spear between their white necks
To drop Cygnus under their hooves.
The aim was perfect,
But the blade, that should have split the sternum,
And the heavy shaft,
That should have carried clean through the body,

Bounced off, like a reed thrown by a boy.
Achilles, astounded, skidded his team to a halt.

Cygnus was laughing.
"I know which goddess was your mother.
The Queen of the Nereids.
But why be surprised if you cannot kill me?
Do you think I wear this helmet
Crested with the tails of horses
For protection? Or that I present this shield
To save my skin? Or tuck myself in a breastplate
Because I am nervous?
I carry these for ornament only,
Just as Mars himself does. Naked,
My skin would still be proof
Against the whole Greek arsenal,
Including yours. This is what it means
To be the son not of a sea-nymph
But of Neptune, lord of the whole ocean
And all its petty deities."
His spear followed his words—
Achilles, with a gesture, caught it
On the boss of his shield.
The bronze could not stop it.
Nine hardened ox-hides behind the bronze
Could not stop it. The tenth ox-hide stopped it.
Achilles shook it off,
And sent a second spear—
Its shaft vibrating in air—
That bounced off Cygnus, as if off the wall of Troy.
A third as heavy, as fast, and as accurate,
Did no better. Cygnus stood open-armed
Laughing to welcome these guests
That knocked on his chest. By now Achilles
Was groaning with anger
Like the bull that pivots in the arena

Among the scarlet cloaks, his tormentors,
Who cannot be pinned down, but flutter away
From every swipe of his points.

Achilles retrieved his failed spears—
And could hardly believe what he found:
The great blades
Sharp and intact as ever.
"What's happened to my strength?" he muttered.
"Is there something about this fellow that has
    spellbound
The power of my arm—
The same arm
That pulled down the wall of Lyrnesus
When I smashed Thebes
Like a pitcher
Full of the blood of the entire populace?
When I dug such trenches with my weapon
The river Caicus drained
Whole nations of their crimson?
Here, too, this arm has slaughtered so many
Their heaped corpses make monuments—pyramids
All along the shore, to remind me
What strength is in it."

As he pondered this, he noticed
Menoetes, one of the Lycians.
Exasperated, to reassure himself,
He hurled a spear, like a yelled oath.
It went through the breastplate of Menoetes
As if through a letter
He happened to be reading.
It drove on,
And clattered the stones beyond as if it had missed—
But splashing them with blood.

As Menoetes—
Like a crocodile straining to get upright—
Beat his brow on the earth towards which he
    crumpled,
Achilles recovered the spear. "This corpse, this spear
And this arm, I have proved, are perfect Achilles.
Now with the help of heaven," he cried, "let Cygnus
Join us in a similar combination."
And he flung the spear—and it travelled
As if along a beam
That passed through the left nipple of the target.
But at a clang the shaft bowed
And sprang off sideways. Nevertheless
At that point of impact a splat of blood
Brought a cry from Achilles—
A cry of joy, ignorant
That what he saw was the blood of Menoetes.
He leapt onto Cygnus like a tiger,
Hacking at him from every direction
With his aerobatic sword.
The flaring helmet flew off in shards
Like the shell of a boiled egg.
And the shield
Seemed to be making many wild efforts
To escape in jagged fragments.
But Achilles' blade
Bit no deeper. With a pang of despair
He saw its edge turning, like soft lead,
As he hewed
At the impenetrable neck sinews
Of this supernatural hero.

With a bellow of fury
He lifted his shield
And slammed the boss full in the face of Cygnus,

Spreading the nose like a crushed pear
And denting the skull-front concave
In a shower of teeth. At the same time
He pounded the top of his skull with the sword
    pommel,
Left, right, left, right, boss and pommel.
Cygnus staggered backwards,
His head on its anvil, under two giant hammers,
His neck-bones splintering, his jawbone lolling to his
    chest.
Terror and bewilderment had already
Removed the world from Cygnus.
A big rock blocked his retreat, he tripped backwards
Splayed across it,
Like a victim on an altar.
And now Achilles hoisted him
By his helpless legs, and whirled his head
Through the vertical arc of his noble height,
Like an axe,
Slam down onto the edged stones.
Then dropped on him, knee staving the rib-cage.
He gripped and twisted the thong—
All that remained of the fled helmet—
Under his chin, a tourniquet that tightened
With the full berserk might of Achilles
Till the head almost came off,
And Cygnus was dead.

Achilles' eyes cleared, as he kneeled there
Panting and cooling.
But now, as he undid the buckles
That linked the corpse's gorgeous armour,
He found his plunder empty.

In those moments
Neptune's word had breathed in off the ocean

And carried away Cygnus
On white wings, their each wingstroke
Yelping strangely—a bird with a long
Undulating neck and a bruised beak
Aimed at a land far beyond the horizon.

Arachne

Minerva, goddess of weavers,
Had heard too much of Arachne.
She had heard
That the weaving of Arachne
Equalled her own, or surpassed it.

Arachne was humbly born. Her father
Laboured as a dyer
Of Phocaean purple. Her mother
Had been humbly born. But Arachne
Was a prodigy. All Lydia marvelled at her.

The nymphs came down from the vines on Tmolus
As butterflies to a garden, to flock stunned
Around what flowered out of the warp and the weft
Under her fingers.
Likewise the naiads of Pactolus

Left sands of washed gold
To dazzle their wonder afresh
On her latest. They swooned at all she did.
Not only as it lay done, but as each inch crept
From under her touches.

A grace like Minerva's, unearthly,
Moved her hands whether she bundled the fleeces
Or teased out the wool, like cirrus,

Or spun the yarn, or finally
Conjured her images into their places.

Surely, only Minerva could have taught her!
Arachne
Laughed at the suggestion.
Her sole instructor, she claimed, was her inborn skill.
"Listen," she cried, "I challenge Minerva

"To weave better than I weave,
And if she wins
Let her do whatever she wants with me,
I shan't care."
Minerva came to Arachne

As an old woman
Panting and leaning on a stick.
"Some things that age brings," she began,
"Are to be welcomed. Old experience teaches
The thread of consequence cannot be broken.

"Listen to my warning. Give to mortals
The tapestries that make you
Famous and foremost among mortal weavers,
But give to the goddess
Your gratitude for the gift.

"Leave it to her to boast of you, if she wants to,
And ask her to forgive you
For your reckless remarks
Against her.
She will hear and she will be merciful."

Arachne turned from her loom.
She reared like a cobra, scowling,
And came near to striking the old woman,

Her eyes hard with fury.
As she spat at her: "Your brain totters

"Like your decrepit body.
You have lived too long.
If you possess daughters or granddaughters
Waste your babble on them.
I am not such a fool

"To be frightened by an owl-face and a few screeches.
I make up my own mind,
And I think as I always did.
If the goddess dare practise what she preaches
Why doesn't she take up my challenge?

"Why doesn't she come for a contest?"
As Arachne spoke, the old woman
Seemed to flare up
To twice her height, crying: "She has come."
All the nymphs fell prostrate.

The women of Mygdonia bowed and hid
Their faces in terror.
Only Arachne brazenly
Defied the goddess, with a glare. She flushed deep red
In the rush of her anger, then paled—

As the dawn crimsons then pales.
But she stuck to her challenge. Too eager
For the greater glory now to be won,
She plunged with all her giddy vanity
Into destruction.

Minerva bent to the contest
Without another word. She rigged up her loom.
The shuttles began to fly.

Both rolled their upper garments down
Under their breasts to give their arms freedom

For every inspiration.
So concentrated on the outcome
Neither was aware how hard she was working,
Feeding the cloth with colours
That glowed every gradation

Of tints in the rainbow
Where the sun shines through a shower
And each hue dissolves
Into its neighbour too subtly
For human eye to detect it.

Minerva portrayed the divine
History of her city, Athens,
And how it came to be named.
There were the twelve high gods surrounding Jove.
She characterised each one:

Jove in his majesty and thunders,
Neptune splitting a crag
With his trident, and the ocean
Gushing from the crevasse—
By which he claimed the city.

And herself, with a shield and a long spear,
The high-ridged helmet on her head
And over her breasts the aegis.
And, where she speared the earth, silvery olives
Springing up, with berries.

The gods gazed astonished. A winged
Victory perfected the assembly.
Then the goddess

Filled each corner with an illustration
Of the kind of punishment

Arachne could now expect for her impudence.
In one corner, two snowy summits,
Rhodope and Haemus, had been human
Before they assumed for themselves
The names of the greatest gods.

In another corner the Queen of the Pygmies
Who had challenged Juno and lost
Had become a crane
Warring against her own people.
In the third corner Antigone,

Who had challenged Juno, cried in vain
To her father Laomedon and to the city of Troy
As the goddess turned her into a stork.
She tries to cheer herself with the white flash
Of her broad wings and her beak's clatter.

In the fourth corner Cinyras
Embraced the temple steps—all that remained
Of his daughter, his tears
Splashing the stones.
Finally

With an embroidered border of tangled olives—
Pallas framed her design
And completed the work
With her own tree, like a flourish,
The tree of peace, an olive.

Arachne's tapestry followed a different theme.
It showed Europa crying from out at sea
Astride the bull that had deceived her.

The high god Jupiter, in his bull form,
Carrying her off—

And glistening with effort.
You could see her feet recoiling
From the swipe of the waves through which he
    heaved.
And Asteria was there
Fighting to keep her clothes on

Under the storming eagle.
And Leda, bared
Under the blizzard of the swan.
Across the growing pattern Jupiter
Varied and multiplied

His amorous transformations:
A satyr
Planted Antiope with her divine twins.
The lady of Tyrins yielded her body
Only to one she thought Amphitryon.

The lap of Danae opened
Only to a shower of gold. Here
The god has gone into the eye of a candle
To comfort Asopus' daughter.
There he's a shepherd, knowing Mnemosyne

Adores that flute.
And there as a freckled serpent
He has overcome Demeter's daughter.
In each of these Arachne
Gave Jove rich new life.

Then moved on to Neptune—
Who had become a great bull, too, to cope

With the daughter of Aeolus.
And as the god of a river
Sweeps Aloeus' wife away in a grasp

That casts her up imprinted with twin sons.
Here a ram
Surprises Bisaltis. There a masterful horse
Circumvents the modesty of Demeter.
A dolphin dives with Melantho. And the curse

Of Medusa's grisly beauty
Softens for a bird.
Arachne captures them all as if she had copied
Each as it happened.
Then she brings on Phoebus—

As a peasant, a falcon, a lion, last as a shepherd
Seducing Isse, Macareus' daughter.
Then Bacchus, with a bunch of grapes
That are no grapes, deceiving Erigone.
And there in the glowing weave,

Saturn a stallion
Begetting Chiron—half man and half pony.
Arachne bordered her picture, to close it,
With a sparkling wreath of cunningly knotted
Flowers and ivy. So it was finished.

And neither the goddess
Nor jealousy herself
Could find a stitch in the entire work
That was not perfection. Arachne's triumph
Was unbearable.

Minerva tore from the loom
That gallery of divine indiscretions

And ripped it to rags.
Then, all her power gone
Into exasperation, struck Arachne

With her boxwood shuttle
One blow between the eyes, then another,
Then a third, and a fourth. Arachne
Staggered away groaning with indignation.
She refused to live

With the injustice. Making a noose
And fitting it round her neck
She jumped into air, jerked at the rope's end,
And dangled, and spun.
Pity touched Minerva.

She caught the swinging girl: "You have been wicked
Enough to dangle there for ever
And so you shall. But alive,
And your whole tribe the same through all time
Populating the earth."

The goddess
Squeezed onto the dangling Arachne
Venom from Hecate's deadliest leaf.
Under that styptic drop
The poor girl's head shrank to a poppy seed

And her hair fell out.
Her eyes, her ears, her nostrils
Diminished beyond being. Her body
Became a tiny ball.
And now she is all belly

With a dot of head. She retains
Only her slender skilful fingers

For legs. And so for ever
She hangs from the thread that she spins
Out of her belly.

Or ceaselessly weaves it
Into patterned webs
On a loom of leaves and grasses—
Her touches
Deft and swift and light as when they were human.

Bacchus and Pentheus

So the fame of the blind
Seer Tiresias
Flared up in all the Greek cities.
Only Pentheus, King of Thebes,
Laughed at the old man's prophecies.
"In-fill for empty skulls,"
He jeered at this dreamer.
"Dreams," he explained,
"Which this methane-mouth
Tells us are the dark manifesto
Of the corrector,
In fact are corpse-lights, the ignes fatui,
Miasma from the long-drop
And fermenting pit
Of what we don't want, don't need,
And have dumped.
They rise from the lower bowel. And lower."
The laughter of Pentheus
Clanged through his malodorous prisons and echoed
Into the underworld and into heaven.

Tiresias replied with his usual riddle:
"How lucky for you, Pentheus,
If only you, like me, had managed
To get rid of your two eyes
That so sharply
Supervise everything and see nothing.

Then you would not have to watch
What Bacchus will do to you.
These dreams, that you miscall ridiculous,
And that attract your derision,
Just as your own dear face
Will be unrecognisable
Because of a glittering mask of blowflies—
These dreams
Have shown me this new god, son of Semele,
And they have shown me a preview, in full colour,
Of a banquet
Bacchus will hold for you, Pentheus,
At which you will be not only guest of honour
But the food and drink. Think of it.
Your expensive coiffure
With your face wrapped in it
Wrenched off like a cork, at the neck,
Your blood
Poured out over your mother and sisters,
Your pedigree carcase
Ripped by unthinking fingers
Into portions, and your blue entrails,
Tangled in thorns and draped over dusty rocks,
Tugged at by foxes.
All this, Pentheus, as clear as if
It had already happened. I saw it
In a silly dream
Which this new god, outlawed by you,
Gave to me on a street corner.
Gave to me—for me to give to you.
What can it mean?"

Pentheus with a roar
Kicked the old blind man
Like a stray befouling dog

From his palazzo. A lifetime too late
To alter himself or his fate.

The god has come. The claustrophobic landscape
Bumps like a drum
With the stamping dance of the revellers.
The city pours
Its entire population into the frenzy.
Children and their teachers, labourers, bankers,
Mothers and grandmothers, merchants, agents,
Prostitutes, politicians, police,
Scavengers and accountants, lawyers and burglars,
Builders, layabouts, tradesmen, con-men,
Scoundrels, tax-collectors, academicians,
Physicians, morticians, musicians, magicians,
The idle rich and the laughing mob,
Stretched mouths in glazed faces,
All as if naked, anonymous, freed
Into the ecstasy,
The dementia and the delirium
Of the new god.

Pentheus rushes about, his voice cracks.
He screams like an elephant:
"This is a disease—
Toads have got into the wells,
The granaries have all gone to fungus,
A new flea is injecting bufotenin.
You forget, you Thebans,
You are the seed of the god Mars.
Remember your ancestry
Under the tongue of the great serpent
Inaccessible to folly.
You veterans, what has happened to your hearing—
It was cured and seasoned

By the crash of weaponry and the war-cries
And the dying cries of the enemy.
How can you go capering
After a monkey stuffed with mushrooms?
How can you let yourselves be bitten
By this hopping tarantula
And by these glass-eyed slavering hydrophobes?
You pioneers, you first settlers, heroes,
You who raised our city, stone by stone,
Out of the slime of the salt marsh,
And hacked its quiet, with your sword's edge,
Out of the very solar system
To shield a night light for your babes and toddlers,
How can you
Go rolling your eyes and waggling your fingers
After that claque of poltroons?
Remember
How often you dragged yourselves, by your teeth and
      nails,
Out of the mass graves
And the fields of massacre,
Clutching your wives and new-born,
Fighting off the hyenas—
Can a fed-back, millionfold
Amplified heartbeat
And some drunken woman's naked heel tossed over
      your heads
Bounce you out of your wits—
Like bobbing unborn babies?
Iron warriors, menhirs of ancient manhood,
Tootling flutes
Wet as spaghetti?
And you philosophers,
Metaphysicians, where are your systems?
What happened to the great god Reason?
And to the stone table of Law

That you fitted back together
Out of the Absolute's shattering anger
Against backsliders?
You have become sots,
You have dunked it all, like a doughnut,
Into a mugful of junk music—
Which is actually the belly-laugh
Of this androgynous, half-titted witch.
You are forgetting the other.
You forget the hard face of the future
With its hungry mouth and its cry
Which is the battle-cry
That waits behind the time of plenty
Hungry for all you have,
And that massacres for amusement, for thrills,
And to liberate your homes and your land
From your possession.
You forget the strangers who are not friendly.
They are coming over the earth's bulge
Out of the wombs of different mothers.
As sure as the moon's tide,
They will lift off your roofs and remove your walls like
      driftwood
And take all you have.
With ground steel they will separate you from it,
Leaving you hugging the burnt earth.
If Thebes has to fall
That would be better.
We could succumb to such a fate with honour.
Then our despair would resemble a noble trophy,
Our tears would be monumental.
But you have surrendered the city
Not to war's elemental chaos
And heroes harder and readier than yourselves
But to a painted boy, a butterfly face,
Swathed in glitter.

A baboon
Got up as an earring
In the ear of a jigging whore.

"As for this lewd, blasphemous joke
About his birth—
Begotten by God himself, a divine by-blow,
Then snatched by his father's scorched fingers
Out of the incineration of his mother—
Sodden, squirming, no bigger than a newt,
Then gestated full term, an implant,
In the thigh of Almighty God.
By which he implies—like a papoose
In God's scrotum.
Do you hear this fairy tale?
How can you swallow it? Bring the juggler to me.
Let me get my thumbs on that Adam's apple,
I'll pop this lie out of him, with squeals,
Like the pip of yellow
Out of a boil. Like a pulp of maggot,
A warble-fly chrysalis
From under the hide of a bull.
Bring him."

With the dry foam framing his lips
Pentheus sent his praetorian guard
To arrest this creature, this Bacchus,
Acclaimed as a new god.

His grandfather, blear-eyed but long-sighted,
Tried to restrain him.
The wise elders, too tottery and arthritic
To go dancing, tried to restrain him.
Their warnings fell like holy water sprinkled
Onto a pan of boiling pig-fat.
Their head-shakings, white-haired, white-bearded,

Like a log-jam in a big river
Only broke his momentum into bellowings,
Frothings, and the plunge
Of a cataract.

The guards come back bruised and dishevelled.
They bring to Pentheus not the Bacchus he wanted
But a different prisoner. They call him
"A priest of the new rites."
Hands bound, a jackal-faced Etruscan.
Pentheus' glare, a white-hot branding iron,
Bears down on the face of this prisoner.
With difficulty he calms
His homicidal hands, as he speaks:
"Your death approaches
Very fast, simply because
Your friends need the warning. So: quickly:
What is your homeland, your family, and your name?
And how does it come about
That you end up here, the manikin doll
Of this ventriloquial, mesmeric,
Itinerant common fraud?"

The voice that answers him is quite fearless.
"I am Acoetes, out of Maeonia.
My parents were poor.
My father possessed neither stock
Nor ground for it to stand on.
His wealth
Was a barbed hook and the art
Of finding fish with it.
These, and the wilderness of waters,
Were his bequest to me.
But I grew weary of wading among herons.
I took to open water.
I pushed a prow out through breakers.

I stretched my cunning
Between the tiller, the sail
And the constellations.
As I learned the moods
Of the menagerie of heaven—
Of squally Capricornus, the saturnine goat,
Of the Hyades, the little piglets
Showering summer stars,
Of the two bears revolving in their clock—
All the winds of ocean
Became familiar, and their safe havens.

"One time,
My destination Delos, I was blown
Onto the coast of Chios.
Skill with the oars got us ashore safely.
That night we camped there. At dawn
I sent Opheltes, the bosun, with men
To find fresh water,
While I climbed a headland
To study the wind, the sky-signs, the horizons.
Everything looked promising. I returned
To the ship, recalling my crew.
'Look what we've found,' shouted Opheltes.
He shoved ahead of him a strange boy,
A little boy, beautiful as a girl.
They'd picked him up on the hillside.
Straight away they'd recognised plunder.
The child staggered,
Mouth half open, eyelids heavy.
He was ready to collapse
With wine, or sleep, or both.
But I saw, I knew, by everything
About him, this boy was more than mortal.
His face, his every movement,
Told me he was a god.

I said to the crew: 'I do not know
Which god you have found but I am certain
This child is divine.'
Then I spoke to the boy: 'Whoever you are,
Preserve our lives in the sea, bless our voyage,
And forgive these fellows
Their rough words and their rough hands.'

" 'None of that rubbish,' cried Dictys. 'This boy's
    ours.'
His anger was quick—like his body,
Quickest of all, like a gibbon,
To hurtle here and there in the ship's rigging.
Lybis roared agreement. He was a dullard.
Always feeling he was being robbed
Or outwitted, always wanting a fight.
Melanthus joined them—he was sharper, our look-out,
But bored with too much emptiness
In front of and behind his blond eyelashes.
Alcemidon likewise. He thought only
Of what he could get away with.
And black Epopus, whose voice was a maul,
Literally, one huge muscle
All to itself, the timekeeper
And metronome of the oarsmen,
Always craving for exercise. And the rest,
They bent their voices to his
Just as out on the sea they bent their bodies.
The girlish boy
Was a landfall, a whole port
For these testy sailors. But I blocked
The top of the gangplank.
'Bestial sacrilege,' I told them,
'Shall not defile this vessel
While I am master of it.'

"The worst man among them pretended to retch.
Lycabus. He was so reckless
He seemed to be searching everywhere
With a kind of desperation
For his own violent death.
Tuscany had thrown him out
For murdering a neighbour.
He grabbed at my throat with his rower's fingers
And would have pitched me overboard
But I caught hold of a rope, and between my knee
And his pelvic bone
Gave his testicles the fright of their lives.
The whole crew bellowed, with one voice,
For him to get up
And finish what he had started.
The uproar
Seemed to rouse the boy.
The great god Bacchus awoke.
'My friends,' he cried,
'What was that awful noise? It sounded awful!
Where am I? How did I get here?
Are you planning to take me somewhere?
Tell me where.'
Proreus found a soft voice.
'Nothing to be afraid of. You seemed lost.
We thought you'd like a lift.
Where do you want to go?
Wherever you say—and we'll drop you off.'
Then the god said:
'Naxos is my home. Take me there
And many friends for life
Will give you a welcome to remember.'

"Those criminals
With sudden hilarity
Swore by the sea and all its gods to take him.

And they urged me to get under way—
To do the boy this easy favour.
I took them at their word
Since Lycabus still sprawled
Groaning and vomiting in the scuppers.
I set the painted prow
Towards Naxos.

"Then Opheltes, in a hissing whisper,
Asked me if I was crazy.
And the rest of the crew, their faces,
Their mouthings, their gestures, made it plain—
They wanted me to take the boy where they pleased,
Very far from Naxos.
I could not believe
They could suppose a god could be tricked by men.
I told them:
'This is not only wicked—it is stupid.
I'll have no part in it.'
Then one of them, Aethalion,
Shouldered me from the helm.
'In that case,' he said, 'leave our fortunes to us.'

"As the ship heeled, the god of actors
Went reeling off balance. He clutched the gunwale,
Stared at the churned swerve in the wake
And pretended to weep.
'This is not the way home,' he wailed.
'The sun should be on that side. We were
Right before. What have I done wrong?
What is the world going to say
If the whole crew of you
Kidnap one small boy?'
Those bandits laughed at his tears
And they laughed at me too, for mine.
But I swear

By the god himself
(And there is no god closer to hear me)
That the incredible
Truly now did happen.

"First, the ship stops dead in the sea
As if rammed into a dry dock.
The oarsmen are amazed. They grimace
And force the blood from under their fingernails
To budge the hull or shear the rowlocks.
The sails are helpless,
Flogging in their ropes. Then suddenly ivy
Comes swarming up the oars, it cumbers the oar-
    strokes
And tumbles in over the deck,
Coiling up the masts, boiling over
To spill great bundles, swinging in the wind,
Draping the sails. And the god
Is standing there, mid-ship, crowned
With clusters of fat grapes.
He brandishes a javelin
Twined with stems and leaves of the vine.
And around him are heaped, as if real,
The great shapes of big cats, yawning, blinking,
The striped and the spotted, leopards, lynxes,
Tigers and jungle cats.

"Then either in panic terror or godsent madness
Every man leaps up, as if for his life,
And overboard into the sea.
Medon was the first to go black.
His spine arched into a half-wheel, mid-air.
Lycabus gibbered at him. 'Look, he's changing
Into a sea-monster—'
As his own gape widened
Backwards beneath his ears, in the long smile

Of a dolphin, and his nose flattened,
His body slicked smooth, his skin toughened.
And Libys—his hands slipped from the oar
Because they were already shrinking.
Before he hit the wave he knew they were fins.
Another was reaching up
To free the ropes from the ivy
And found he had no arms. With a howl
He somersaulted over the stern
In a high arc
Flailing the black half-moon of a dolphin tail
That was suddenly his.
These creatures crash round the ship.
They fling sheets of spray over the ivy
As they plunge under. Or they burst upwards
Like a troupe of acrobatic dancers—
Blasting out in a fume, through their blowholes,
The sea they gulp as they frolic.
I was the survivor of twenty,
Shuddering with fear, barely sane.
But the god was kind.
'Now steer towards Dia,' he told me.
And I did so. And there I was rewarded.
I entered the priesthood of this mighty god."

Now Pentheus spoke:
"You have dreamed us a long dream,
With a deal of ocean bluster,
But my anger has neither slept nor cooled."
He called for slaves.
"Break this man on the rack elaborately.
Send him down to hell grateful
For the respite."

So Acoetes was dragged off, and slammed
Into a strongroom.

But it is told:
While the executioner's implements
Of fire, pincers, choppers, and incidentals,
Were being readied
To gratify Pentheus, of a sudden
Bolts shot out of their sockets and went skittering
Over the floors. Locks exploded
In a scatter of components curiously fractured.
Doors flew open untouched.
And untouched the shackles
Fell off Acoetes.

Pentheus heard of this. But from it
Learned nothing. Instead, his brain temperature
Rose a degree. Something insane
Behind his eyes
Tore off its straitjacket.
He thought no more of bodyguards
Than of jailors, warders, doctors, nurses.
Alone he climbed Cithaeron,
The mountain consecrated to Bacchus,
Where the air
Pounded his eardrums like mad fists
And seemed to pound in his heart,
And the screaming songs of the possessed
Were like the screams of a horse, reverberating
Inside the horse's own skull.
Pentheus was like that horse
On a battlefield, when the unfought fury
Shimmers in mid-air before the attack,
And the blast of the trumpets
Goes like lightning
Through every supercharged nerve,
And he whinnies, rolls his eyeballs,
Champs foam and paws at the far sky
To be first at the enemy—

Pentheus was like that
When he heard the unbearable howls
And ululations
Of the Bacchantes, and the clash of their cymbals.
And when he stumbled in his fury
And fell on all fours,
When he clutched the sod and felt their stamping
Shaking the mountain beneath his fingers,
When Pentheus
Saw the frightened worms
Twisting up out of their burrows
Then the red veil came over his vision.

Halfway up the slope is a level clearing.
Pentheus bounded into the open
And halted—
Utterly unprepared
For what he had surprised.
He stared, in a stupor,
Into the naked mysteries.

The first to see him,
The first to come for him
Like a bear defending her cubs,
The first to drive her javelin into him
Was his own mother—
Screeching as she came:
"It's the boar that ploughed up our gardens!
I've hit it! Quickly, sisters, now we can kill it!
I've hit it." Pentheus falls
And the whole horde of women
Pile on top of him
Like a pack of wild dogs,
Like a squabbling heap of vultures.
Every one claws to get hold of something
And pull it away.

A changed man, Pentheus,
Emptied with terror,
Tries to crawl.
His mouth bites at new words,
Strange words, words that curse himself,
That renounce himself, that curse Pentheus.
He convicts himself,
Begs for forgiveness
With blood coming out of his mouth.
He heaves upright,
Shouting to his aunt: "Autonoë,
Remember your darling Actaeon
Torn to rags by the hounds that loved him.
Pity me." The name Actaeon
Sounds to her like the scream of a pig
As she wrenches his right arm
Out of its socket and clean off.
While Ino, with the strength of the god,
Twists the other likewise clean off.
Armless, he lurches towards his mother.
"Mother," he sobs, "Mother, look at me,
Recognise me, Mother!"
Agave stares, she blinks, her mouth wide.
She takes her son's head between her hands
And rips it from his shoulders.
She lifts it, like a newborn baby,
Her red fingers hooked into the hair
Letting the blood splash over her face and breasts—
"Victory!" she shrieks. "I've done it! I did it!"

Swiftly, like a light breeze at dawn,
After the first hard night-frost of the year
Has left a tree's leaves
Numbed and precariously clinging,
So swiftly

The hands of those women
Separated the King's bones and stripped them.

The lesson
Was not lost on Thebes, the city of letters.
Women made sure, thereafter,
That this sleepy child
Was acknowledged, was honoured
And made happy by all who played with him
In his ritual play,
Blessing all who blessed him.

Midas

Peasants crowded to gawp at Silenus—
The end-product of a life
They could not imagine.
They chained him with flowers and dragged him,
In a harness of flowers, to their King, Midas,
As if he were some
Harmless, helpless, half-tapir or other
Charming monster.
When Midas recognised him,
And honoured him, fat and old and drunk as he was,
As the companion of Bacchus,
And restored him to the god,

Bacchus was so grateful
He offered to grant Midas any wish—
Whatever the King wanted, it would be granted.
Midas was overjoyed
To hear this first approach, so promising,
Of his peculiar horrible doom.
He did not have to rack his brains.
A certain fantasy
Hovered in his head perpetually,
Wistfully fondled all his thoughts by day,
Manipulated all his dreams by night.
Now it saw its chance and seized his tongue.
It shoved aside
The billion—infinite—opportunities

For Midas
To secure a happiness, guaranteed,
Within the human range
Of what is possible to a god.
It grasped, with a king's inane greed,
The fate I shall describe.

Midas said: "Here is my wish.
Let whatever I touch become gold.
Yes, gold, the finest, the purest, the brightest."
Bacchus gazed at the King and sighed gently.
He felt pity—
Yet his curiosity was intrigued
To see how such stupidity would be punished.
So he granted the wish, then stood back to watch.

The Phrygian King returned through the garden
Eager to test the power—yet apprehensive
That he had merely dreamed and now was awake,
Where alchemy never works. He broke a twig
From a low branch of oak. The leaves
Turned to heavy gold as he stared at them
And his mouth went dry.
He felt his brain move strangely, like a muscle.
He picked up a stone and weighed it in his hand
As it doubled its weight, then doubled it again,
And became bright yellow.
He brushed his hand over a clump of grass,
The blades stayed bent—soft ribbons
Of gold foil. A ripe ear of corn
Was crisp and dry and light as he plucked it
But a heavy slug of gold, intricately braided
As he rolled it between his palms.
It was then that a cold thought seemed to whisper.
He had wanted to chew the milky grains—
But none broke chaffily free from their pockets.

The ear was gold—its grain inedible,
Inaccessibly solid with the core.
He frowned. With the frown on his face
He reached for a hanging apple.
With a slight twist he took the sudden weight
No longer so happily. This was a fruit
He made no attempt to bite, as he pondered its
    colour.

Almost inadvertently he stroked
The door pillars, as he entered the palace,
Pausing to watch the brilliant yellow
Suffuse the dark stone.
He washed his hands under flowing water, at a
    fountain.
Already a hope
Told him that the gift might wash away,
As waking up will wash out a nightmare.
But the water that touched him
Coiled into the pool below as plumes
Of golden smoke, settling heavily
In a silt of gold atoms.

Suddenly his vision
Of transmuting his whole kingdom to gold
Made him sweat—
It chilled him as he sat
At the table
And reached for a roasted bird. The carcase
Toppled from his horrified fingers
Into his dish with a clunk,
As if he had picked up a table ornament.
He reached for bread
But could not break
The plaque of gold that resembled a solid puddle
Smelted from ore.

Almost in terror now
He reached for the goblet of wine—
Taking his time, he poured in water,
Swirled the mix in what had been translucent
Rhinoceros horn
But was already common and commoner metal.
He set his lips to the cold rim
And others, dumbfounded
By what they had already seen, were aghast
When they saw the wet gold shine on his lips,
And as he lowered the cup
Saw him mouthing gold, spitting gold mush—
That had solidified, like gold cinders.
He got up, reeling
From his golden chair, as if poisoned.

He fell on his bed, face down, eyes closed
From the golden heavy fold of his pillow.
He prayed
To the god who had given him the gift
To take it back. "I have been a fool.
Forgive me, Bacchus. Forgive the greed
That made me so stupid.
Forgive me for a dream
That had not touched the world
Where gold is truly gold and nothing but.
Save me from my own shallowness,
Where I shall drown in gold
And be buried in gold.
Nothing can live, I see, in a world of gold."

Bacchus, too, had had enough.
His kindliness came uppermost easily.
"I return you," said the god,
"To your happier human limitations.
But now you must wash away

The last stain of the curse
You begged for and preferred to every blessing.
A river goes by Sardis. Follow it upstream.
Find the source
Which gushes from a cliff and plunges
Into a rocky pool. Plunge with it.
Go completely under. Let that river
Carry your folly away and leave you clean."

Midas obeyed and the river's innocent water
Took whatever was left of the granted wish.
Even today the soil of its flood plain
Can be combed into a sparse glitter.
And big popcorns of gold, in its gravels,
Fever the fossicker.

Midas never got over the shock.
The sight of gold was like the thought of a bee
To one just badly stung—
It made his hair prickle, his nerves tingle.
He retired to the mountain woods
And a life of deliberate poverty. There
He worshipped Pan, who lives in the mountain caves.
King Midas was chastened
But not really changed. He was no wiser.
His stupidity
Was merely lying low. Waiting, as usual,
For another chance to ruin his life.

—

The cliff-face of Tmolus watches
Half the Mediterranean. It falls away
To Sardis on one side, and on the other
To the village of Hypaepa.
Pan lives in a high cave on that cliff.

He was amusing himself,
Showing off to the nymphs,
Thrilling them out of their airy bodies
With the wild airs
He breathed through the reeds of his flute.
Their ecstasies flattered him,
Their words, their exclamations, flattered him.
But the flattered
Become fools. And when he assured them
That Apollo, no less,
Stole his tunes and rearranged his rhythms
It was a shock
For Pan
To find himself staring at the great god
Hanging there in the air off the cave mouth,
Half eclipsed with black rage,
Half beaming with a friendly challenge.
"Tmolus, the mountain," suggested the god, "can
         judge us."

Tmolus shook out his hair,
Freed his ears of bushes, trees, birds, insects,
Then took his place at the seat of judgement,
Binding his wig with a whole oak tree—
The acorns clustering over his eyebrows,
And announced to Pan: "Your music first."

It so happened
Midas was within hearing
Collecting nuts and berries. Suddenly he heard
Music that froze him immobile
As long as it lasted. He did not know
What happened to him as Pan's piping
Carried him off—
Filled him with precipices,
Lifted him on weathered summits,

Poured blue icy rivers through him,
Hung him from the stars,
Replaced him
With the fluorescent earth
Spinning and dancing on the jet of a fountain.

It stopped, and Tmolus smiled,
As if coming awake—
Back, he thought, hugely refreshed
From a journey through himself.
But now he turned
To Apollo, the great, bright god.
As he turned, all his forests
Dragged like a robe.

Apollo was serious.
His illustrious hair burst
From under a wreath of laurel picked
Only moments ago on Parnassus.
The fringe of his cloak of Tyrian purple
Was all that touched the earth.
In his left hand the lyre
Was a model, in magical code,
Of the earth and the heavens—
Ivory of narwhal and elephant,
Diamonds from the interiors of stars.
In his right hand he held
The plectrum that could touch
Every wavelength in the Universe
Singly or simultaneously.
Even his posture
Was like a tone—like a tuning fork,
Vibrant, alerting the whole earth,
Bringing heaven down to listen.

Then the plectrum moved and Tmolus,
After the first chords,
Seemed to be about to decompose
Among the harmonics.
He pulled himself together—but it was no use,
He was helpless
As the music dissolved him and poured him
Through the snakes and ladders
Of the creation and the decreation
Of the elements,
And finally, bringing the sea-horizon
To an edge clean as a knife,
Restored him to his shaggy, crumpled self.

Pan was humbled. Yes, he agreed—
Apollo was the master. Tmolus was correct.
The nymphs gazed at Apollo. They agreed.
But then a petulant voice,
A hard-angled, indignant, differing voice
Came from behind a rock.

Midas stood up. "The judgement," he cried,
"Is ignorant, stupid, and merely favours power.
Apollo's efforts
Are nothing but interior decoration
By artificial light, for the chic, the effete.
Pan is the real thing—the true voice
Of the subatomic."

Apollo's face seemed to writhe
Momentarily
As he converted this clown's darkness to light,
Then pointed his plectrum at the ears
That had misheard so grievously.

Abruptly those ears lolled long and animal,
On either side of Midas' impertinent face.
Revolving at the root, grey-whiskered, bristly,
The familiar ears of a big ass.
The King,
Feeling the change, grabbed to hang on to his ears.
Then he had some seconds of pure terror
Waiting for the rest of his body to follow.
But the ears used up the power of the plectrum.
This was the god's decision. The King
Lived on, human, wagging the ears of a donkey.

Midas crept away.
Every few paces he felt at his ears and groaned.
He slunk back to his palace. He needed
Comfort. He was bitterly disillusioned
With the spirit of the wilderness.
He hid those ears—in a turban superb
As compensation could be.

But a king needs a barber.
Sworn to secrecy or impalement
The barber, wetting his lips,
Clipped around the gristly roots
Of the great angling ears as if the hair there
Might be live nerve-ends.
What he was staring at,
And having to believe, was worse
For him than for their owner,
Almost. He had to hide this news
As if it were red-hot
Under his tongue, and keep it there.
The ultimate shame secret
Of the ruler of the land.
It struggled to blurt
Itself out, whenever

He opened his mouth.
It made him sweat and often
Gasp aloud, or strangle
A groan to a sigh. Or wake up
In the middle of the silent night
Certain he had just
Yelled it out, at the top of his voice,
To the whole city.
He knew, this poor barber,
He had to get it out somehow.

In the lawn of a park he lifted a turf
After midnight. He kneeled there
And whispered into the raw hole,
"Ass's ears! Midas has ass's ears!"
Then fitted the turf back, trod flat the grave
Of that insuppressible gossip,
And went off, singing
Under his breath.

But in no time,
As if the barber had grafted it there
From some far-off reed-bed,
A clump of reeds bunched out, from that very sod.
It looked strange, on the park lawn,
But sounded stranger.
Every gust brought an articulate whisper
Out of the bending stalks. At every puff
They betrayed the barber's confidence,
Broadcasting the buried secret.
Hissing to all who happened to be passing:
"Ass's ears! Midas has ass's ears!"

Niobe

Niobe had known Arachne.
She, too, scorned the gods—
For a different reason. Arachne's fate
Taught Niobe nothing.
Niobe was proud. She was proud

Of the magical powers of her husband—
Amphion, the King. And she was proud
Of the purity of the noble blood
They both shared. And proud
Of their kingdom's envied might and splendour.

But above all these, her greatest pride
Was her family—her fourteen children.
And it is true, Niobe, of all mothers
Would have been the most blest
If only she had not boasted

That she, of all mothers, was the most blest.

The daughter of Tiresias, Manto,
Whose prophetic frenzy
Opened the three worlds to her,
Came raving into the streets, possessed by vision.
She screamed at the women of Thebes:

"The goddess is speaking through my mouth.
She commands you all:
Twist laurels round your heads, gather at the temple,
Burn incense—give prayers and offerings
To Leto and the children of Leto."

The Theban women asked no questions.
If that was what the goddess wanted
That is what they would give her.
They filled the temple, their worshipping cries went up
To Leto and the children of Leto.

But suddenly, in a swirl of attendants,
Niobe was among them.
She looked magnificent—
Like a great flame, in her robes of golden tissue.
She reared her spectacular head,

Her hair coiled and piled like a serpent
Asleep on a heap of jewels.
Anger made her beauty awesome.
From her full height she raked the worshippers
With a glare of contempt.

"Isn't this insane?
Aren't you all out of your minds
To offer tributes to these gods in the sky
Who exist only by hearsay?
How can you do this

"And at the same time ignore
Real divinity such as your eyes can see?
You worship Leto
Who lives only in a story
At altars built specially for her.

"But who has built an altar to acknowledge
What is divine in me?
My father was Tantalus—
Among all mortals only he
Sat at the feasts of the gods.

"Only he clinked glasses with them. My mother
Is a sister of the Pleiades.
And that great god among the greatest, Atlas,
Who bears the globe of heaven on his back—
He is my grandfather. And who forgets

"That my grandfather on the other side
Is Jupiter himself?
And it is no boast
When I remind you that great Jupiter
Is also my father-in-law.

"All Phrygia kneels and pays homage
To me. I rule over this city
That rose into place, stone by stone,
As if weightless, obedient
To my husband's magical airs.

"I am the Queen of the Royal Palace of Cadmus.
Wherever my eyes rest in my house
They rest on fabulous wealth.
Nor can it be denied—my own beauty
Is not equalled on any face in heaven.

"No—I have been blessed above all women.
Who can deny it? Who can doubt
That my great fortune will continue to grow?
It is too great—far, far too great
For Fate to reverse.

"Ill-fortune
Cannot lay a finger on me.
Let her take whatever she will—
Whatever she can take, still she leaves me
Far more than she takes.

"Tell me,
How can I fear ill-fortune?
Even if it came to the worst—
If I lost some of my children—
I could never be left with only two.

"Only two!
Two is all that Leto ever had.
Two children! You might as well have none.
Get rid of these laurels. Back to your homes.
Finish with this nonsense. Finish, I say."

Cowed, the women of Thebes obeyed her.
They dropped the laurel wreaths, broke off their
    worship,
Left the altars—
But their prayers to Leto, like
Subterranean rivers, could not

Be stopped or diverted.
They flowed on, unspoken, heard only by Leto.
And Leto was enraged.
She climbed to the top of Cynthus
And cried out to her children—the twins:

None other than Apollo and Diana,
So lightly dismissed by the Phrygian Queen.
"Your mother is calling you," she cried.
"Your mother, who is so proud of being your mother.
In heaven I take second place to none

"Except Juno herself. Hear me, my children.
Your mother's divinity is being denied.
Women loyal to me from the beginning
Are forbidden to worship at my altar.
Niobe has forbidden it. Oh, help me.

"The daughter of Tantalus has inherited
All her father's blasphemous folly.
Not only has she emptied my temples,
She drives me mad
With insults, derision,

"And tells the whole world her fourteen children
Are a thousand times superior
To my two. Compared to her I am childless.
O my children, double her mockery—back
Into her own mouth, let her swallow its meaning."

Leto would have gone on
But her great son Apollo spoke: "Mother,
Your words merely prolong Niobe's delusion."
He exchanged a signal with his sister.
Together they sailed through the sky

Like an eclipse in a cloud
Till they hung over the city of Cadmus.

Outside the city
A broad plain smoked like a burning ground,
Pounded bare and hard
By charioteers and horsemen, to and fro
Exercising their horses.
Niobe's sons were out there
Astride gaudy saddle-cloths,
Their gold-studded reins bunched in their fingers,
Managing muscular horses.

Ismenus, Niobe's eldest,
Was reining his horse hard,
Bringing it round in a tight circle
When his spine snapped
And a bellow forced his mouth open
As a broad-headed bright-red arrow
Came clean through him.
The reins fell loose. For a moment
He embraced the horse's neck, limply,
Then slid from its right shoulder.

Sipylus looked wildly upward.
He heard a quiver rattle high in the air
And urged his horse to a full gallop—
As the ship's pilot
Seeing the overtaking squall behind him
Puts out every inch of canvas
To catch every breath and escape it—
But it was no good.
The god's arrow was already there,
The feathers squatting in the nape of his neck,
The long shaft sticking from his Adam's apple.
He bowed
Over the horse's mane and simply
Rolled on forward and down
Under the hooves
That churned his limbs briefly, scattering the blood.

Phaedimus was no luckier.
With his brother—
Who had inherited the ominous name
Of his grandfather, Tantalus—
He had left the horses. These two
Were doing what they loved best—
Wrestling together, with oiled bodies,
And were locked chest to chest,

Each straining to fold the other backwards
When the arrow
From the unerring bow of Apollo
Slammed through both, and nailed them together.
Each thought his backbone broken by the other.
With a single groan they collapsed,
Crumpling sideways
A monster with eight limbs, clawing for life,
Dying a single death from the one wound.

Alphenor could not understand
What was happening.
He hammered his chest with his fists and tore at it
With his fingers. He tried
To lift his two brothers back on their feet—
But as he struggled there, with all his strength
Braced under their dead weights,
A forked barb of Apollo
Touched him beneath his left shoulder-blade.
It came out under his ribs, on the right,
With a rag of his liver.
He felt his heart kicking against the shaft
As he dropped into darkness
Beneath his brothers.

Long-haired Damasichthon was not so lucky
To escape so smoothly.
The arrow that brought him down
Had gone in behind the knee.
He flung back his head,
Showing heaven a mask of agony
As he made one huge effort to wrench
The barbs from their anchorage
Behind his tendons.
The second arrow found him in that posture.
It went in

At the base of his throat, in the fork
Of his clavicle—
And drove straight down through the aorta.
A column of blood
Ejected it and he fell
Like a broken fountain—
The blood jetting in twisting and showering arcs
From his flailing body.

Ilioneus was last.
He dropped to his knees and lifted his arms—
"You gods," he cried, "all of you, hear me,
Spare me, protect me."
But ignorant of his mother's folly
He was ignorant
Which gods to appeal to.

Apollo the Archer, touched with pity,
Regretted the arrow
That his eye was following.
But the wound was instantly fatal,
Surgical, precise, minimal—
It stopped his heart before he felt the impact.

Now the news came looking for Niobe.
Rumour like an electrical storm-wind
Whisking the dust at street corners—
People huddling together, then scattering
In an uproar of wails. Till at last
Her own family burst in on her, shrieking.

She heard it unable to believe—
Knowing it all true,
As the severed limb cannot feel.
Astounded that the gods could do so much
So swiftly,

Aghast that they had the power to do it,
Enraged that they had dared.

The final blow fell on her
As if she were already senseless.
Amphion, her husband, hearing the news
Had stabbed himself, ending his grief with his life.

This was no longer Niobe the Queen
Who had driven her people, as with a whip,
From Leto's altars,
Who had stalked through her own city
Like a conqueror
Viewing a conquest—
When her beauty, her pride, her arrogance
Sickened the people with envy and hatred.

Now even those who hated her most
Pitied her. She bowed
Over the cooling bodies of her sons.
She kissed them, as if she could give them
A lifetime of kisses in these moments.
She lifted her bruised arms:
"Leto," she cried, "feast yourself
On your triumph, which is my misery.
I have died seven deaths—at your hands.
In each of these seven corpses I died
In agony and lie dead.
Gloat. And exult. And yet
Your victory is petty.
Though you have crushed me I am still far, far
More fortunate than you are.
I still have seven children."
Demented with her losses,
Niobe no longer knew
How to be frightened or prudent.

And even as she spoke
Terror struck
With an invisible arrow
All who heard
A bowstring thud in the air.

The seven sisters of the dead brothers
Stooped by the seven biers,
Loose hair over their shoulders, mourning.
One of them, as she eased
The arrow from the heart of her brother,
Fell on him,
An arrow through her own,
Already dead, her mouth on his mouth.

Another, consoling her mother,
Stopped mid-sentence, bent
Over her sudden wound and collapsed,
Mouth closed and eyes vacant.
Another, running, seemed to stumble—
But her sprawl was lifeless.
Another tripping over her body
Was dead in the air as she fell.
One of them
Squeezed her head and shoulders
Under a dead brother, another
Stood in the open sobbing,
Paralysed with fear.

When six of them lay dead
Niobe grabbed the seventh and covered her
With her limbs and body,
And tried to protect her
In swathes of her robes, crying:
"Leave me my youngest.
Leave me one. Leave me the smallest.

Of all my children let me keep this one."
But a slender arrow
Had already located
The child
She tried to hide and pray for.

Niobe gazed at the corpses.
All her children were dead.
Her husband was dead.
Her face hardened
And whitened, as the blood left it.
Her very hair hardened
Like hair carved by a chisel.
Her open eyes became stones.
Her whole body
A stone.

Life drained from every part of it.
Her tongue
Solidified in her stone mouth.
Her feet could not move, her hands
Could not move: they were stone,
Her veins were stone veins.
Her bowels, her womb, all stone
Packed in stone.
And yet
This stone woman wept.

A hurricane caught her up
And carried her
Into Phrygia, her homeland,
And set her down on top of a mountain.
And there, a monument to herself,
Niobe still weeps.
As the weather wears at her
Her stone shape weeps.

Salmacis and Hermaphroditus

Among those demi-gods, those perfect girls
Who sport about the bright source and live in it,
The beauty of Salmacis, the water-nymph,
Was perfect,
As among damselflies a damselfly's,
As among vipers the elegance
Of a viper, or a swan's grace among swans.
She was bending to gather lilies for a garland
When she spied Hermaphroditus.
At that first glimpse she knew she had to have him.
She felt she trod on prickles until she could touch him.
She held back only a moment,
Checked her girdle, the swing of her hem, her
     cleavage,
Let her lust flood hot and startled
Into her cheek, eyes, lips—made her whole face
Open as a flower that offers itself,
Wet with nectar. Then she spoke:
"Do you mind if I say—you are beautiful?
Seen from where I stand, you could be a god.
Are you a god? If you are human,
What a lucky sister! As for the mother
Who held you, and pushed her nipple between your
     lips,
I am already sick with envy of her.
I dare not think of a naked wife in your bed.
If she exists, I dare not think of her bliss.

Let me beg a taste, one little sip
Of her huge happiness. A secret between us.
But if you are unmarried—here I am.
Let us lie down and make our own
Bridal bed, where we can love each other
To sleep. And awaken each other."

The boy blushed—he had no idea
What she was talking about.
Her heart lurched again when she saw
How his blush bewildered his beauty.
Like the red side of an apple against a sunset,
Or the ominous dusky flush
That goes over the cold moon
When the eclipse grips its edge
And begins to swallow it inch by inch
In spite of all the drums and pans and gongs
Beaten on earth beneath to protect it.

Then the nymph slid her arms
Around his neck, and asked for a kiss,
One kiss, one brotherly kiss—
"Get away," he cried. "Let me go,
Or I'm off. And you can sit here
On your basket of tricks all by yourself!"
That scared Salmacis, she thought he really might go.
"Oh no, forgive me!" she sobbed. "Forgive me!
I couldn't help it. I'm going. Oh, I'm spoiling
This lovely place for you. I'm going. I'm going."

So, lingering her glances, she goes,
And truly she seems to have gone.
In fact, she has ducked behind a bush.
There she kneels, motionless, head lifted—
Her eye fixed, like the eye of a leopard.
He plays, careless as a child,

Roams about happily
Thinking he's utterly alone.
He paddles into the pool's edge, goes deeper.
The cool pulse of the spring, warping the clarity,
Massages his knees, delicious.
He peels off his tunic and the air
Makes free with all that had been hidden,
Freshens his nudity. Under the leaves
Salmacis groaned softly
And began to tremble.
As the sun
Catches a twisting mirror surface
With a splinter of glare
Her own gaze flamed and hurt her. She was already
Up and leaping towards him,
She had grabbed him with all her strength—
Yet still she crouched where she was
Shaking all over, letting this go through her
Like a dreadful cramp. She watched him
Slap his pale shoulders, hugging himself,
And slap his belly to prepare it
For the plunge—then plunge forward.
And suddenly he was swimming, a head bobbing,
Chin surging through the build of a bow-wave,
Shoulders liquefied,
Legs as if at home in the frog's grotto,
Within a heave of lustre limpid as air
Like a man of ivory glossed in glass
Or a lily in a bulb of crystal.

"I've won!" shrieked Salmacis. "He's mine!"
She could not help herself.
"He's mine!" she laughed, and with a couple of
        bounds
Hit the pool stark naked
In a rocking crash and thump of water—

The slips of her raiment settling wherever
They happened to fall. Then out of the upheaval
Her arms reach and wind round him,
And slippery as the roots of big lilies
But far stronger, her legs below wind round him.
He flounders and goes under. All his strength
Fighting to get back up through a cloud of bubbles
Leaving him helpless to her burrowing kisses.
Burning for air, he can do nothing
As her hands hunt over him, and as her body
Knots itself every way around him
Like a sinewy otter
Hunting some kind of fish
That flees hither and thither inside him,
And as she flings and locks her coils
Around him like a snake
Around the neck and legs and wings of an eagle
That is trying to fly off with it,
And like ivy which first binds the branches
In its meshes, then pulls the whole tree down,
And as the octopus—
A tangle of constrictors, nippled with suckers,
That drag towards a maw—
Embraces its prey.

But still Hermaphroditus kicks to be free
And will not surrender
Or yield her the least kindness
Of the pleasure she longs for,
And rages for, and pleads for
As she crushes her breasts and face against him
And clings to him as with every inch of her surface.
"It's no good struggling," she hisses.
"You can strain, wrestle, squirm, but cannot
Ever get away from me now.
The gods are listening to me.

The gods have agreed we never, never
Shall be separated, you and me."

The gods heard her frenzy—and smiled.

And there in the giddy boil the two bodies
Melted into a single body
Seamless as the water.

Tereus

Pandion, the King of Athens, saw
King Tereus was as rich
And powerful as himself.
He was also descended from the god Mars.
So Pandion gave his daughter to Tereus,
And thought himself happy.

Hymen and Juno and the Graces,
Those deities who bless brides, shunned this marriage.
Instead the bridal bed was prepared by the Furies
Who lit the married pair to it with torches
Stolen from a funeral procession.
Then an owl

Flew up from its dark hole to sit on the roof
Directly above their bed. All that night
It interrupted their joy—
Alternating little mewing cries
With prophetic screams of catastrophe.
And this was the accompaniment of omens

When Tereus, the great King of Thrace,
Married Procne, and begot Itys.
But all Thrace rejoiced. Thereafter,
The day of their wedding and the Prince's birthday
Were annual jubilees for the whole nation.
So ignorant are men.

Five years passed. Then Procne spoke to her husband,
Stroking his face. "If you love me
Give me the perfect gift: a sight of my sister.
Let me visit her. Or, better still,
Let her visit us. Go—promise my father
Her stay here can be just as brief as he pleases."

At a command from Tereus, oar and sail
Brought him to Athens. There King Pandion
Greeted his son-in-law. Tereus
Began to explain his unexpected arrival—
How Procne longed for one glimpse of her sister.
But just as he was promising

The immediate return of Philomela
Once the two had met, there, mid-sentence,
Philomela herself—arrayed
In the wealth of a kingdom—entered:
Still unaware that her own beauty
Was the most astounding of her jewels.

She looked like one of those elfin queens
You hear about
Flitting through the depths of forests.
Tereus felt his blood alter thickly.
Suddenly he himself was like a forest
When a drought wind explodes it into a firestorm.

She was to blame—her beauty. But more
The King's uncontrollable body.
Thracians are sexually insatiable.
The lust that took hold of him now
Combined the elemental forces
Of his national character and his own.

His first thought was: buy her attendants
And her nurses with bribes.
Then turn the girl's own head
With priceless gifts—
Cash in your whole kingdom for her.
His next thought was

Simply to grab her
And carry her off—
Then fight to keep her. He was the puppet
Of instant obsession. No insane plan
Gave him pause if it promised to make her his.
All of a sudden, wildly impatient

He pressed Pandion again with Procne's request—
The glove of his own greed. Passion
Made him persuasive. When he went too far
He swore Procne
Sickened to see her sister.
He even wept as he spoke,

As if he had brought her tears with him
As well as her pleading words.
God in heaven, how blind men are!
Everybody who witnessed it marvelled
At what this man would do for his wife's sake,
The lengths he would go to! And yet

The acting was irresistible!
Philomela was overwhelmed. She wept too,
Hugging her father, pleading through her tears.
As he loved her and lived for her happiness
She begged him to grant her this chance—
The worst that any woman ever suffered.

Tereus stared at the Princess,
Imagining her body in his arms.
His lust
Was like an iron furnace—first black,
Then crimson, then white
As he watched her kiss and caress her father.

He wished himself her father—
In which case
His intent would have been no less wicked.
King Pandion surrendered at last
To the doubled passion of his daughters.
Ecstatic, Philomela

Wept and thanked him for his permission
As if he had bestowed
Some enormous gift on her and her sister,
Rather than condemned them, as he had,
To the fate
That would destroy them both.

The sun went down.
A royal banquet glittered and steamed.
The guests, replete, slept.
Only the Thracian King, Tereus, tossed,
Remembering Philomela's every gesture,
Remembering her lips,

Her voice, her hair, her hands, her glances,
And seeming to see
Every part her garments concealed
Just as he wanted it.
So he fed his lust and stared at the darkness.
Dawn lit the wharf at last

For their departure. Now King Pandion
Implored his son-in-law to guard his charge:
"I lend her to you
Because you and she and her sister were persuasive.
By your honour, by the gods, by the bond between
        us,
Protect her like a father.

"Send her home soon,
This darling of my old age.
Time will seem to have stopped till I see her again.
Philomela, come back soon, if you love me.
Your sister's absence alone is more than enough."
The King embraced his daughter and wept.

Then asked both—Tereus and the girl—
To give him their hands, as seals of their promise.
He joined their hands together—
Beseeching them to carry his blessing
To his far-off daughter and his grandson.
There the father choked

On his goodbye.
His voice collapsed into sobs,
Overwhelmed of a sudden
By fear—
Inexplicable, icy,
A gooseflesh of foreboding.

The oars bent and the wake broadened
Behind the painted ship.
Philomela watched the land sinking
But Tereus laughed softly:
"I've won. My prayers are granted. She is mine."
He was in a fever for the delights

That he deferred only with difficulty.
And the nape of her neck was aware
Of his eyes
As he gloated on her—like an eagle
That has hoisted a hare in its gripe
To its inescapable tower.

The moment the ship touched his own shore
Tereus lifted Philomela
Onto a horse, and hurried her
To a fort, behind high walls,
Hidden in deep forest.
And there he imprisoned her.

Bewildered and defenceless,
Failing to understand anything
And in a growing fear of everything,
She begged him to bring her to her sister.
His answer was to rape her, ignoring her screams
To her father, to her sister, to the gods.

Afterwards, she crouched in a heap, shuddering—
Like a lamb still clinging to life
After the wolf has savaged it
And for some reason dropped it.
Or like a dove, a bloody rag, still alive
Under the talons that stand on it.

Then like a woman in mourning
She gouged her arms with her nails,
She clawed her hair, and pounded her breasts with her
      fists,
Shrieking at him: "You disgusting savage!
You sadistic monster!
The oaths my father bound you to—

Were they meaningless?
Do you remember his tears—you are inhuman,
You couldn't understand them.
What about my sister waiting for me?
What about me?
What about my life?
What about your marriage?
You have dragged us all
Into your bestial pit!
How can my sister think of me now?
Your crime is only half done—
Kill me and complete it.
Why didn't you kill me first
Before you destroyed me that other way?
Then my ghost at least
Would have been innocent.
But the gods are watching—
If they bother to notice what has happened—
If they are more than the puffs of air
That go with their names—
Then you will answer for this.
I may be lost,
You have taken whatever life
I might have had, and thrown it in the sewer,
But I have my voice.
And shame will not stop me.
I shall tell everything
To your own people, yes, to all Thrace.
Even if you keep me here
Every leaf in this forest
Will become a tongue to tell my story.
The dumb rocks will witness.
All heaven will be my jury.
Every god in heaven will judge you."

Tereus was astonished
To be defied and raged at and insulted
By a human being. And startled
By the sudden clutch of fear
As her words went home. Speechless, mindless,
In a confusion of fear and fury

He hauled her up by the hair,
Twisted her arms behind her back and bound them,
Then drew his sword.
She saw that
As if she were eager, and bent her head backwards,
And closed her eyes, offering her throat to the blade—

Still calling to her father
And to the gods
And still trying to curse him
As he caught her tongue with bronze pincers,
Stretched it out to its full length and cut it
Off at the root.

The stump recoiled, silenced,
Into the back of her throat.
But the tongue squirmed in the dust, babbling on—
Shaping words that were now soundless.
It writhed like a snake's tail freshly cut off,
Striving to reach her feet in its death-struggle.

After this, again and again—
Though I can hardly bear to think about it,
Let alone believe it—the obsessed King
Like an automaton
Returned to the body he had mutilated
For his gruesome pleasure.

Then, stuffing the whole hideous business
Deep among his secrets,
He came home, smooth-faced, to his wife.
When she asked for her sister, he gave her
The tale he had prepared: she was dead.
His grief, as he wept, convinced everybody.

Procne stripped off her royal garments
And wrapped herself in black. She built a tomb
Without a body, for her sister,
And there she made offerings to a ghost
That did not exist, mourning the fate of a sister
Who endured a fate utterly different.

A year went by. Philomela,
Staring at the massive stone walls
And stared at by her guards, was still helpless,
Locked up in her dumbness and her prison.
But frustration, prolonged, begets invention,
And a vengeful anger nurses it.

She set up a Thracian loom
And wove on a white fabric scarlet symbols
That told in detail what had happened to her.
A servant, who understood her gestures
But knew nothing of what she carried,
Took this gift to Procne, the Queen.

The tyrant's wife
Unrolled the tapestry and saw
The only interpretation
Was the ruin of her life.
She sat there, silent and unmoving,
As if she thought of something else entirely.

In those moments, her restraint
Was superhuman. But grief so sudden, so huge,
Made mere words seem paltry.
None could lift to her lips
One drop of its bitterness.
And tears were pushed aside

By the devouring single idea
Of revenge. Revenge
Had swallowed her whole being. She had plunged
Into a labyrinth of plotting
Where good and evil, right and wrong,
Forgot their differences.

Now came the festival of Bacchus
Celebrated every third year
By the young women of Thrace.
The rites were performed at night—
All night long the din of cymbals
Deafened the city.

Dressed as a worshipper
Procne joined the uproar. With a light spear,
Vine leaves round her head, and a deer pelt
Slung over her left shoulder, she became
A Bacchante, among her attendants. Berserk
She hurled herself through the darkness, terrifying,

As if possessed by the god's frenzy.
In fact, she was crazy with grief.
So she found the hidden fort in the forest.
With howls to the god, her troop tore down the gate,
And Procne freed her sister, disguised her
As a Bacchante, and brought her home to the palace.

Philomela felt she might die
Of sheer fear, when she realised
She was in the house of her ravisher.
But Procne,
Shut in the safety of her own chamber,
Bared her sister's face and embraced her.

Philomela twisted away.
Shame tortured her.
She would not look at her sister—
As if she herself were to blame
For the King's depravity.
She fixed her eyes on the ground like a madwoman.

While her gestures flailed
Uselessly to tell the gods all
That Tereus had done to her
Doubling his cruelty on her body,
Despoiling her name for ever.
Procne took her shoulders and shook her.

She was out of her mind with anger:
"Tears can't help us,
Only the sword
Or if it exists
Something more pitiless
Even than the sword.

"O my sister, nothing now
Can soften
The death Tereus is going to die.
Let me see this palace one flame
And Tereus a blazing insect in it,
Making it brighter.

"Let me break his jaw. Hang him up
By his tongue and saw it through with a broken knife.
Then dig his eyes from their holes.
Give me the strength, you gods,
To twist his hips and shoulders from their sockets
And butcher the limbs off his trunk

"Till his soul for very terror scatter
Away through a thousand exits.
Let me kill him— Oh! However we kill him
Our revenge has to be something
That will appal heaven and hell
And stupefy the earth."

While Procne raved Itys came in—
Her demented idea
Caught hold of his image.
"The double of his father," she whispered.
Silent, her heart ice,
She saw what had to be done.

Nevertheless as he ran to her
Calling to her, his five-year-old arms
Pulling at her, to be kissed
And to kiss her, and chattering lovingly
Through his loving laughter
Her heart shrank.

Her fury seemed to be holding its breath
For that moment
As tears burned her eyes. She felt
Her love for this child
Softening her ferocious will—and she turned
To harden it, staring at her sister's face.

225   [*Tereus*

Then looked back at Itys
And again at her sister, crying:
"He tells me all his love—but she
Has no tongue to utter a word of hers.
He can call me mother, but she
Cannot call me sister.

"This is the man you have married!
O daughter of Pandion!
You are your father's shame and his despair.
To love this monster Tereus, or pity him,
You must be a monster.
It is monstrous!"

Catching Itys by the arm she gave herself
No more time to weaken.
Like a tiger on the banks of the Ganges
Taking a new-dropped fawn
She dragged him into a far cellar
Of the palace.

He saw what was coming. He tried
To clasp her neck screaming: "Mama, Mama!"
But staring into his eyes
Procne pushed a sword through his chest—
Then, though that wound was fatal enough,
Slashed his throat.

Now the two sisters
Ripped the hot little body
Into pulsating gobbets.
The room was awash with blood
As they cooked his remains—some of it
Gasping in bronze pots, some weeping on spits.

A feast followed. Procne invited
One guest only, her husband.
She called it a ritual
Peculiar to her native land
And special for this day, when the wife
Served her lord, without attendant or servant.

Tereus, ignorant and happy,
Lolled on the throne of his ancestors
And swallowed, with smiles,
All his posterity
As Procne served it up. He was so happy
He called for his son to join him:

"Where is Itys? Bring him."
Procne
Could not restrain herself any longer.
This was her moment
To see him fall helpless onto the spike
In the pit she had dug for him.

"Your son," she said, "is here, already.
He is here, inside,
He could not be closer to you."
Tereus was mystified—
He suspected some joke, perhaps Itys
Was hiding under his throne.

"Itys," he called again. "Come out,
Show yourself." The doors banged wide open,
Philomela burst into the throne-room,
Her hair and gown bloody. She rushed forward,
And her dismembering hands, red to the elbows,
Jammed into the face of Tereus

A crimson, dripping ball,
The head of Itys.
For moments, his brain
Refused to make sense of any of it.
But the joy she could not speak
Philomela released in a scream.

Then it was his turn.
His roar tore itself
Out of every fibre in his body.
He heaved the table aside—
Shouting for the Furies
To come up out of hell with their snake-heads.

He tugged at his rib-cage,
As if he might rive himself open
To empty out what he had eaten.
He staggered about, sobbing
That he was the tomb of his boy.
Then gripped his sword-hilt and steadied himself

As he saw the sisters running.
Now his bellow
Was as homicidal
As it was anguished.
He came after them and they
Who had been running seemed to be flying.

And suddenly they were flying. One swerved
On wings into the forest,
The other, with the blood still on her breast,
Flew up under the eaves of the palace.
And Tereus, charging blind
In his delirium of grief and vengeance,

No longer caring what happened—
He too was suddenly flying.
On his head and shoulders a crest of feathers,
Instead of a sword a long curved beak—
Like a warrior transfigured
With battle-frenzy dashing into battle.

He had become a hoopoe.
Philomela
Mourned in the forest, a nightingale.
Procne
Lamented round and round the palace,
A swallow.

Pyramus and Thisbe

Throughout the East men spoke in awe of Thisbe—
A girl who had suddenly bloomed
In Babylon, the mud-brick city.

The house she had grown up in adjoined
The house where Pyramus, so many years a boy,
Brooded bewildered by the moods of manhood.

These two, playmates from the beginning,
Fell in love.
For angry reasons, no part of the story,

The parents of each forbade their child
To marry the other. That was that.
But prohibition feeds love,

Though theirs needed no feeding. Through signs
Their addiction to each other
Was absolute, helpless, terminal.

And the worse for being hidden.
The more smothered their glances, the more
Agonised the look that leapt the gap.

In the shared wall that divided their houses,
Earth-tremors had opened a fissure.
For years, neither household had noticed.

But these lovers noticed.
Love is not blind. And where love cannot peer
Pure clairvoyance whispers in its ear.

This crack, this dusty crawl-space for a spider,
Became the highway of their love-murmurs.
Brows to the plaster, lips to the leak of air

And cooking smells from the other interior,
The lovers kneeled, confessing their passion,
Sealing their two fates with a fracture.

Sometimes they slapped the wall, in frustration:
"How can a wall be so jealous!
So deaf to us, so grudging with permission!

"If you can open this far for our voices
Why not fall wide open, let us kiss,
Let us join bodies as well as voices.

"No, that would be too much. That would mean
The wall repaired to part us utterly.
O wall, we are grateful. Nowhere in the world

"But in this tiny crack may our great loves,
Invisibly to us, meet and mingle."
Then each would kiss the crack in the cold plaster,

Their own side of the wall, with a parting kiss.
This could not go on for long.
One day at their confessional, they decided

To obey love and risk everything.
They made their plan: that night they would somehow
Escape from their guarded houses,

Leave the city, and tryst in the open country—
Their rendezvous the mulberry tree
Over the tomb of Ninus, a famous landmark.

At this time of the year the tree was loaded
With its milk-white fruit, that a cool spring
Made especially plump and succulent.

Their plan enthralled them—with the joy it promised.
A promise that seemed so sure
No possible snag or snarl, no shadow of an error,

No shiver of apprehension troubled it.
Their sole anxiety was the unrelenting
Glare of the sun in the day, that seemed to have
    stopped.

But suddenly it was dark.
Thisbe had oiled the hinges. Now they helped her
Slip from the house like the shadow of a night-bird

Leaving the house-eaves. The moonlight
That lit her path from the city
Found the sparks of her eyes, but not her pallor—

Her veil hid all but her eyes from night watchers.
So she came to the tomb. Sitting in the shadow
Of the tree dense with fruit

That reflected the moon, like new snow,
She stared out into the brilliant jumble
Of moonlight and shadows. She strained

To catch the first stirring of a shadow
That would grow into Pyramus. It was then,
As she peered and listened,

And felt the huge silence, the hanging weight
Of the moonlit cliff above her,
And, above the cliff, the prickling stars,

That the first fear touched her.
She froze, her breath shrank, slight as a lizard's.
Only her eyes moved.

She had seen, in her eye-corner, a shadow
That seemed to have shifted.
Now she could hear her heart. Her head swivelled.

Somebody was walking towards her.
She stood, she leaned to the tree, her legs trembling.
She realised she was panting.

And almost cried out: "Pyramus!"
But at that moment
The shadow coughed a strange cough—hoarse,
        cavernous,

And was much nearer, moving too swiftly.
A strangely hobbling dwarf, bent under something.
Then her brain seemed to turn over.

Plain in the moonlight she saw
That what had looked like a dwarf
Was nothing of the kind. Slouching

Directly towards her
Under its rippling shoulders, a lioness
Was coming to wash its bloody jaws,

And quench its hanging belly, its blood-salt surfeit,
In the spring beside her.
Without another thought, Thisbe was running—

She left her veil floating
To settle near the water. She ran, ducking
Behind the tomb of Ninus, too frightened to scream,

And squeezing her eyes shut, squeezed herself
Into a crevice under the cliff.
The lioness drank, then found the veil,

The perfumed veil perfumed again
By a woman's excitement, and her fear.
The beast began to play with the veil—

Forepaws tore downwards, jaw ripped upwards.
And the veil towelled the blood
From the sodden muzzle, and from the fangs.

Soon the beast lost interest
In this empty skin, so savourless,
And the beautiful weave was abandoned.

The lioness went off. She was absorbed
Among the moonlit rocks
As if she had never happened. Only the veil

Waited for Pyramus
Who now emerged running, his shadow vaulting
        beside him.
Both stopped at the spring.

The lion's footprints, alien, deep, unwelcome,
Printed the spring's margin.
Pyramus picked up the veil, too familiar

Blackened by blood though it was—
Blood so fresh and glistening. He groaned,
Not unlike the lioness

But groaning words: "Did our planning
Foresee this double death as a fitting
Finale to our love which was forbidden?

"But Thisbe should have escaped the lion and lived.
I am to blame—for appointing this wild place
But failing to be here before her."

Then he roared aloud: "Are there any more lions
Living in the cliff there?
Come out and punish a criminal."

He groaned again, to himself:
"Cowards call for death—but courage
Does something about it."

He swayed, weeping into the sticky remnant:
"Let our blood mingle
As never in love, in this veil torn by a lion."

He set his sword point to his chest
And ran at the tree, burying the blade to the hilt,
Then with his last effort pulled it from the wound.

When a lead conduit splits, the compressed water
Jets like a fountain.
His blood shot out in bursts, each burst a heartbeat,

Showering the fruit of the tree—
Till the white fruits, now dyed hectic purple,
Dripped his own blood back onto his body

That spilled the rest of its life, in heavy brimmings,
To the tree roots that drank it
And took it up to the fruits, that fattened darker.

Thisbe's fear for Pyramus and the lion,
And, almost worse, the thought that he might have
        arrived
And be at the tomb without her

Brought her running. But when she saw
The tree that had been snow-white with its fruit
Now purple-dark, blackish in the moonlight,

Her new fear was that she had lost her bearings
And come to the wrong place. Then she heard
A grunting cough in the tree's shadow

And saw the body sprawl, as if in sleep,
Into the moonlight.
Now she screamed. Unafraid of the lion

Again and again she screamed.
She embraced his corpse, fierce as any lion,
More passionately than she had ever dreamed

Of embracing it in life. She screamed to him
To wake up and speak to her.
His eyes opened a moment, but death

Was closing their light as they gazed at her.
Thisbe looked down at her hand, it was clutching
The soggy rag of her veil.

She saw his scabbard empty. "It was your love
That persuaded your own hand to kill you.
My love is as great, my hand as ready.

"Once I am with you
My story can be told: the cause of your death,
But your consolation for ever.

"Death has divided us, so it is right
That death should bring us together
In an unbreakable wedlock. Parents,

"As you find our bodies,
Limbs entwined, stiffened in a single knot,
Do not separate us. Burn us as we lived

"In the one flame.
And you who live on, with your boughs laden,
Over two stripped of their blossom, their seed and
        their life,

"Remember how we died. Remember us
By the colour of our blood in your fruit.
So when men gather your fruit, and crush its ripeness,

"Let them think of our deaths."
She spoke, then set the point of the warm sword
Beneath her breast and fell on it.

With her last strength she wound him with her arms
        and legs.

The gods were listening and were touched.
And the gods touched their parents. Ever after
Mulberries, as they ripen, darken purple.

And the two lovers in their love-knot,
One pile of inseparable ashes,
Were closed in a single urn.

GLOSSARY OF

NAMES AND PLACES

[Compiled by Jessica Levenstein]

ACHAIA   Region of the northern Peloponnese; often a name for all
   of Greece

ACHELOUS   Longest Greek river, and its god; his daughters were
   the Sirens—half-women, half-birds, with irresistible voices

ACHERON   River in southern Epirus, the traditional entrance to
   Hades; also its god, the father of Ascalaphus with Orphne

ACHILLES   Son of Peleus, a mortal, and Thetis, a Nereid; the most
   illustrious Greek hero of the Trojan War; killed Hector and was
   killed by Paris, Hector's brother

ACOETES   Maeonian (Lydian) sailor and priest of Bacchus; called
   an Etruscan—one of an ancient Italian people said by Herodotus
   to have come from Lydia

ACTAEON   A hunter; grandson of Cadmus and son of Autonoë and
   Aristaeus

ADONIS   Son of Cinyras and Myrrha, loved by Venus for his great
   beauty

AEACUS   Son of Jupiter and Aegina, father of Peleus, and ruler of
   Aegina

AEGEON   A sea-god

AEGINA   Island in the Aegean Sea, named for Aegina, daughter of
   Asopus and mother of Aeacus by Jupiter

AEOLUS   (1) God of the winds; (2) ancient figure with many chil-
   dren; one of his daughters, thought to be Canace, was loved by
   Neptune in the form of a bull

AETOLIA   Mountainous region in west central Greece

AGAVE   Daughter of Cadmus, mother of Pentheus, and follower of
   Bacchus

241

ALCMENE Daughter of Electryon, King of Tiryns, in Argolis; also called Tirynthia after her birthplace; wife of Amphitryon and mother of Hercules by Jupiter

ALOEUS A giant, son of Neptune; his wife, Iphimedia, was the mother of twins by Neptune

ALPHEUS Largest river in the Peloponnese, and its god

AMATHUS City in Cyprus, sacred to Venus

AMAZONS Female warriors of Scythia or Asia Minor; one of Hercules' twelve labors was to obtain the girdle of the Amazon queen, Hippolyta

AMPHION King of Thebes; twin son (with Zethys) of Antiope and Jupiter, husband of Niobe, and father of her fourteen children

AMPHITRYON King of Thebes; husband of Alcmene

AMYMONE Maiden seduced in Argos by Neptune, who named a spring in her honor

ANAPUS Husband of Cyane

ANTAEUS Libyan giant; son of Neptune and Earth, he derived his strength from contact with his mother

ANTIGONE Daughter of Laomedon, King of Troy; her beauty rivaled Juno's

ANTIOPE Daughter of Nycteus; mother of twins, Amphion and Zethys, by Jupiter disguised as a satyr

APHRODITE Greek name for Venus, the goddess of love

APOLLO Son of Jupiter and Leto, and twin brother of Diana; god of the sun and of music, poetry, and medicine; father of Phaethon and the Heliades; also called Phoebus

ARACHNE A Lydian weaver; the class Arachnida was named for her

ARCADIA Mountainous region in central Peloponnese named for Arcas, and associated with idealized rustic simplicity; a traditional setting for pastoral poetry; an Arcadian boar was slain on Mount Erymanthus by Hercules as one of his twelve labors

ARCAS Son of Callisto by Jupiter disguised as Diana

ARETHUSA Achaian nymph and follower of Diana; also the fountain on the island of Ortygia, site of Syracuse, Sicily, into which the nymph was changed

ARGOLIS   Territory surrounding Argos

ARGOS   City in the Peloponnese protected by Juno; often a name for all of Greece

ARTEMIS   Greek name for Diana, goddess of the hunt

ASCALAPHUS   Son of Orphne and Acheron

ASOPUS   River-god and father of Aegina

ASTERIA   Sister of Leto; pursued by Jupiter in the form of an eagle, she turned into a quail

ASTRAEA   Daughter of Jupiter and Themis; goddess of justice; she lived on earth during the Golden Age (the age of Astraea), but in the Iron Age human depravity drove her away to heaven; she was set among the constellations, under the name of Virgo

ATALANTA   Huntress and athlete of great beauty

ATHENA   Greek name for Minerva; patron of Athens

ATHOS   Mountain in northeastern Greece

ATLAS   Titan, son of Iapetus and Clymene; entrusted with the weight of the heavens, which he bore on his shoulders; father of the Pleiades and the Hyades, and grandfather of Niobe

AUGUSTUS   First Roman emperor; named Octavius at birth, he was adopted by his great-uncle Julius Caesar and made his heir; after Caesar's death and civil war, he became sole ruler of Rome, with the title Augustus, and ruled for forty-one years; Ovid wrote during his reign

AUSTER   South wind

AUTOLYCUS   Son of Mercury (Greek: Hermes) and Chrone; husband of Erysichthon's daughter, and the maternal grandfather of Ulysses (Greek: Odysseus)

AUTONOË   A follower of Bacchus; daughter of Cadmus, sister of Agave, and aunt of Pentheus

AVERNUS   Lake in Italy surrounded by dark woods and known for its sulfurous waters; an entrance to the underworld

BABYLON   City in Mesopotamia, on the Euphrates River, capital of Babylonia

BACCHANTES   Female followers of Bacchus prone to ecstatic, sometimes violent behavior

BACCHIAE   (More commonly Bacchiadae) Family named after

Bacchis, a Corinthian king; its members ruled Corinth for a century and settled throughout the ancient world

BACCHUS (Greek: Dionysus) God of wine, and divine leader of a religion marked by delirium and intoxication; son of Jupiter and Semele; and associated with Thebes

BASSARIDS (Also Bacchantes) Followers of Bacchus named for Bassareus, another name for Bacchus

BISALTIS Raped by Neptune in form of a ram, she bore the ram with the golden fleece

BOEOTIA Country in central Greece

BOÖTES Constellation in the northern sky; the name means "ox-driver"

BOREAS North wind

BUSIRIS Egyptian King who slaughtered all visitors to Egypt; he was killed by Hercules

CADMUS Founder of Thebes; grandson of Neptune, son of the Phoenician king Agenor, brother of Europa, husband of Harmonia (daughter of Mars and Venus), and father of Semele, Ino, Agave, and Autonoë

CAESAR Julius Caesar, Roman statesman and military leader who became sole ruler of the Roman world until his assassination in 44 B.C.

CAICUS River in western Asia Minor

CALLISTO Daughter of Lycaon, and a follower of Diana

CALYDON City in Aetolia; its king, Meleager, invited many of Greece's greatest heroes to hunt an enormous boar sent by Diana to ravage the land

CAYSTER River in Lydia, Asia Minor, renowned for its swans

CENAEUM Promontory in northwest Euboea

CENCHREIS Wife of Cinyras and mother of Myrrha

CENTAURS Creatures, half-man and half-horse, that dwelt in the mountains of Thessaly

CEPHISUS (More commonly Cephissus) River in Boeotia and its god, the father of Narcissus

CERASTAE Tribe of horned people in Cyprus who made sacrifices of their guests

CERBERUS   Three-headed guard dog of the underworld; one of Hercules' twelve labors was to bring Cerberus to the upper world

CERES   (Greek: Demeter) Goddess of agriculture; daughter of Saturn and Ops, sister of Jupiter, and mother of Proserpina by Jupiter

CHIOS   Island in the Aegean Sea, off the coast of Asia Minor, known for its fruit and wines

CHIRON   A centaur fathered by Saturn and renowned for wisdom and learning; teacher of Jason, Achilles, and Asclepius

CILICIA   Region on the southeast coast of Asia Minor

CINYRAS   (1) King of Cyprus; son of Paphos, husband of Cenchreis, and father of Myrrha; unwittingly seduced by Myrrha, he fathered Adonis; (2) unknown figure whose daughter was transformed into the steps of Juno's temple as punishment for her impiety

CITHAERON   Mountain between Boeotia and Attica, and the site of Bacchic rites

CLYMENE   Daughter of Oceanus and Tethys, wife of Merops, and mother of Phaethon by Apollo and of Atlas and Prometheus by Iapetus

CNIDOS   Greek city in Caria, southwest Asia Minor, sacred to Venus

CORINTH   Greek city in the northeast Peloponnese, strategically located on the Isthmus and near the Gulf of Corinth

CUPID   (Greek: Eros) Son of Venus, and god of love, which he enkindles by shooting arrows at his victims

CYANE   Fountain-nymph of Sicily

CYBELE   Phrygian goddess, mother of the gods, whose cult became popular in Rome

CYCLADES   Islands surrounding Delos in the Aegean Sea; the Greek name means "encircling"

CYCLOPES   (Singular: Cyclops) One-eyed giants who forged thunderbolts in heaven; the most famous of the Cyclopes was Polyphemus, son of Neptune, who lived in Sicily and was blinded by Ulysses

CYGNUS   (Also Cycnus) Trojan son of Neptune whose father's divinity made him invulnerable to Achilles' spear

CYLLENE   Highest mountain in Arcadia

CYNTHUS   Mountain on Delos said to be the birthplace of Apollo and Diana, and thus sacred to them; they were thus also known as Cynthius and Cynthia

CYPRUS   Large island in the eastern Mediterranean, near Asia Minor, sacred to Venus

CYTHERA   Island in the Aegean Sea, sacred to Venus, who was often called Cytherea

DANAE   Daughter of Acrisius, King of Argos; impregnated by Jupiter in the form of a golden shower, she gave birth to Perseus

DEIANIRA   Sister of Meleager, King of Calydon, and wife of Hercules

DELOS   Small island in center of the Cyclades; the birthplace of Apollo and Diana, and sacred to Apollo

DEMETER   (Latin: Ceres) Goddess of agriculture; raped by Neptune in the form of a horse; her daughter was Persephone (Latin: Proserpina)

DIA   (More commonly Naxos) Largest island of the Cyclades

DIANA   (Greek: Artemis) Goddess of the moon and the hunt; daughter of Jupiter and Leto, and twin sister of Apollo; a virgin, with a loyal band of virgins who are devoted to her

DINDYMA   (More commonly Dindymus) Mountain in Phrygia, sacred to Ceres

DIOMED   (Abbreviation of Diomedes) Thracian king; son of Mars and Cyrene; one of Hercules' twelve labors was to capture his man-eating horses

DIRCE   Spring in Boeotia, near Thebes, and its water-nymph

DORIS   Sea-goddess; daughter of Oceanus and Tethys, wife of Nereus, and mother of the Nereids

DRYADS   Wood nymphs; each tree had a dryad inhabiting it

EARTH   Goddess, called Gaia in Greek and Terra in Latin; mother and wife of Saturn and mother of the Titans

ECHO   Nymph whom Juno deprived of the ability to speak for herself, so that she could only repeat the words of others

ELIS   Region in northwest Peloponnese renowned for the horses bred there; the stables of Augeus, which Hercules cleansed as one of his twelve labors, were located there

ENNA   City in central Sicily

EPHYRE   Ancient name for Corinth

EPIDAURUS   City in northeast Argolis, in the Peloponnese, known for the worship of Asclepius or Aesculapius, son of Apollo and god of healing

EPIRUS   Region of northwest Greece

ERIDANUS   Ancient name of the river Po

ERIGONE   Daughter of Icarus whom Bacchus pursued in the guise of a grape cluster; she hung herself in grief over her father's death, and was transformed into the constellation Virgo

ERYMANTHUS   (1) River flowing between Arcadia and Elis; (2) mountain in Arcadia

ERYSICHTHON   Son of King Triopas of Thessaly; he felled trees sacred to Ceres

ERYX   Mountain in western Sicily, sacred to Venus

ETNA   (Also Aetna) Volcano in eastern Sicily; when it erupts, Typhon, the giant pinned beneath Sicily, was said to be vomiting ashes; also said to be the workshop of Vulcan

EUBOEA   Large island in the Aegean Sea, just off the eastern coast of Greece

EUPHRATES   River passing through ancient Babylon, in Mesopotamia, and the longest river in southwestern Asia

EUROPA   Daughter of Agenor, King of Phoenicia, and sister of Cadmus; her abduction and rape by Jupiter in the form of a bull is a favorite subject in the classical arts

EUROTAS   River in southeastern Peloponnese that flows past Sparta

EURUS   East wind

EURYSTHEUS   Mycenean king of Argos; descendant of Perseus; through the enmity of Juno toward Hercules, he was made master of Hercules and imposed the twelve labors upon him

EVENUS   (More commonly Euenus) River in Aetolia, near Calydon

FATES   Three female deities, the daughters of Jupiter and Themis, goddess of justice; said to determine the events of each mortal's life inalterably with a thread that they spun, twisted, and finally cut short

FURIES   (Greek: Erinyes) Three divine sisters who lived in hell and avenged evildoing, especially wrongs committed against a person's own kindred

GARGAPHIE   Vale in Boeotia, sacred to Diana, and its spring

GRACES   Three beautiful, divine daughters of Jupiter and Eurynome, a sea-nymph, who presided over kindness and good acts generally

HAEMONIA   A name for Thessaly and northern Greece; the Haemonian archer: the constellation Sagittarius, which was the centaur Chiron, placed by Jupiter among the stars

HAEMUS   Mountain range in Thrace, now called the Balkan Mountains; once a man in love with Rhodope; they were both turned into mountains for their impiety

HECATE   Goddess of enchantments, known for sorcery and black magic

HECTOR   Trojan hero, oldest son of King Priam; his great conflict with Achilles is related in the *Iliad*

HELIADES   Daughters of Apollo and Clymene, and sisters of Phaethon; after his death they were turned into trees whose resin turned to amber

HELICON   Mountain in Boeotia, sacred to Apollo and home of the Muses

HERCULES   (Greek: Heracles) Greek hero, son of Jupiter and Alcmene; performed twelve supposedly impossible labors set for him by Eurystheus

HERMAPHRODITUS   Son of Mercury and Venus (Greek: Hermes and Aphrodite, hence his name)

HESPERUS   Meaning "western": the home of the Hesperides, the nymphs of the evening; an island in the far west, where a tree, guarded by a dragon, bore golden apples; one of Hercules' twelve labors was to pluck these apples

HIPPOMENES   Son of Megareus and grandson of Neptune

HISTER   Ancient name for the Danube River

HOURS (Horae: Latin) Attendants of Phoebus Apollo who per-
    sonified the changing seasons

HYADES Cluster of seven stars in Taurus, originally seven nymphs,
    daughters of Atlas, and sisters of the Pleiades; they were said to
    bring wet weather when they rise and set with the sun

HYDRA Venomous, many-headed snake dwelling in Lerna, a
    swamp in Argolis; one of Hercules' twelve labors was to kill it

HYLLUS Son of Hercules and Deianira

HYMEN The god of marriage; without his presence at the nuptials,
    a marriage was doomed

HYPAEPA Small town in Lydia, Asia Minor

ICARUS (More commonly Icarius) Father of Erigone; when he
    welcomed Bacchus, he was given the vine and the knowledge of
    how to make wine, which he shared with his neighbors; they
    killed him, thinking themselves poisoned, and he became the
    constellation Boötes

IDA (1) Mountain in Phrygia, near Troy, revered by worshippers
    of Cybele; (2) highest mountain in Crete, where Jupiter was
    raised

INO Daughter of Cadmus, and sister of Semele, Agave, and
    Autonoë

IOLE Daughter of Eurytus, King of Oechalia, in Euboea; loved
    by Hercules, after his death she married Hyllus, his son with
    Deianira

ISMARUS Mountain in Thrace known for its wine

ISMENUS (1) River in Boeotia, near Thebes; (2) Niobe's oldest
    son

ISSE Daughter of Macareus (son of Aeolus)

ITYS Son of Tereus and Procne

JOVE Alternate name for Jupiter

JUNO (Greek: Hera) Queen of the gods; daughter of Saturn and
    Ops, sister and wife of Jupiter, and mother of Mars and Vulcan;
    goddess of marriage and childbirth, and intent on punishing her
    husband's mortal lovers

JUPITER (Greek: Zeus) King of the gods; son of Saturn and Ops, brother and husband of Juno, brother of Neptune and Pluto; lover and father of gods and mortals alike; called Jove, the Father, the Thunderer, God, and the Almighty

LAMPETIE   One of the Heliades; daughter of Apollo and Clymene, and sister of Phaethon and Phaethusa

LAOMEDON   King of Troy; father of Priam and Antigone

LEDA   Wife of Tyndareus, King of Sparta; seduced by Jupiter in the form of a swan, she bore two sets of twins: her sons Castor and Pollux (who were set in the sky as the constellation Gemini), and her daughters Helen, wife of Menelaus, and Clytemnestra, wife of Agamemnon

LETO   (Also Latona) Daughter of the Titans Coeus and Phoebe, and mother of twins, Apollo and Diana, by Jupiter

LILYBAEUM   Promontory at the extreme west of Sicily; the legs of Typhon, the giant buried under the island, lay beneath it

LIRIOPE   Water-nymph and mother of Narcissus by Cephisus

LUCINA   Goddess of childbirth; her name means "she who brings to the light"

LYCAEUS   Mountain in Arcadia, sacred to Jupiter

LYCAON   Early king of Arcadia and father of Callisto; visited by Jupiter, he doubted the god's divinity

LYCIA   Mountainous country in southwest Asia Minor

LYCORMAS   River in Aetolia whose sands were known for their golden color

LYDIA   Country in western Asia Minor

LYRNESUS   Small town in Mysia

MACAREUS   King in Lesbos, the largest island off the western coast of Asia Minor; son of Aeolus and father of Isse

MAENALUS   Mountain range in Arcadia

MAEONIA   Older name for Lydia

MANTO   Daughter of Tiresias who has his gift for prophecy

MARS   (Greek: Ares) God of war; son of Jupiter and Juno, lover of Venus, and father of Harmonia (wife of Cadmus) and Diomedes, among others

MEANDER   (Also Maeander) Winding river in western Asia Minor

MEDUSA   A Gorgon; snake-haired female monster whose gaze turns men to stone; raped by Neptune, she bore the winged horse Pegasus

MEGAREUS   Son of Neptune and father of Hippomenes

MELANTHO   Sea-nymph seduced by Neptune in the form of a dolphin

MELAS   River in Thrace

MELEAGER   Calydonian king, brother of Deianira

MEROPS   King of Ethiopia and husband of Clymene

MIDAS   Phrygian king whom Bacchus granted the power to turn everything he touched into gold; the power was taken away when he bathed in the waters of the Pactolus River

MIMAS   Mountain range in Ionia, western Asia Minor

MINERVA   (Greek: Pallas Athena) Virgin goddess of wisdom and technical skill, and herself a skilled weaver; the daughter of Jupiter, she sprang from his head fully armed

MNEMOSYNE   A Titan, daughter of Saturn and Ops, mother of the Muses by Jupiter, and the personification of memory

MOLOSSIANS   (Also Molossi) Tribal people in Epirus, in northwest Greece

MYCALE   Mountainous promontory in Ionia, in western Asia Minor

MYGDONIA   Another name for Phrygia

MYRRHA   Daughter of Cinyras and Cenchreis and mother of Adonis

MYSIA   Country in northwestern Asia Minor

NARCISSUS   Beautiful son of Cephisus and Liriope

NAXOS   (Also Dia) Largest island of the Cyclades, in the Aegean Sea, known for its wines and the worship of Bacchus

NEMEA   Valley in Argolis where Hercules killed a lion as one of his twelve labors

NEMESIS   Daughter of the goddess Night; divine personification of retribution and righteous indignation who punished mortal presumption and pride

NEPTUNE   (Greek: Poseidon) God of the seas and of earthquakes;

son of Saturn and Ops, brother of Jupiter and Pluto, father of Pegasus, Cygnus, Antaeus and others, and grandfather of Megareus

NEREIDS   Fifty sea-nymphs, daughters of Nereus and Doris, who attended greater gods of the sea, especially Neptune; among them were Amphitrite, wife of Neptune, and Thetis

NEREUS   God of the sea, known for his wisdom; son of Oceanus and Tethys, husband and brother of Doris, and father of the Nereids

NESSUS   Centaur; son of Ixion, a Thessalian king who was condemned to whirl eternally on a fiery wheel in Hades for attacking Juno

NINUS   Assyrian king married to Semiramis, Queen of Babylon

NIOBE   Daughter of Tantalus, granddaughter of Atlas and Jupiter, sister of the Pleiades, wife of Amphion, King of Thebes, and mother of seven sons and seven daughters

OECHALIA   City in Euboea, governed by Eurytus, and destroyed by Hercules after Eurytus refused him his daughter, Iole

OETA   Mountain range between Thessaly and Aetolia

OLYMPUS   Mountain between Macedonia and Thessaly, and the highest mountain on the Greek peninsula; home of the gods

OPHIUSA   Older name for Cyprus

OPS   Goddess of the abundance of the earth; identified with the Greek goddess Rhea; wife of Saturn, and mother of many Olympian gods

ORCHOMENUS   City in Arcadia

ORONTES   Chief river of Syria

ORPHEUS   Thracian bard, whose music could rouse emotion in wild beasts, trees, and mountains; son of the Muse Calliope by either Apollo or Oeagrus, a king of Thrace; husband of Eurydice; after her death he wandered through the mountains of Thrace, playing his lyre

ORPHNE   Nymph married to Acheron, and mother of Ascalaphus

ORTYGIA   Island on which the oldest part of the city of Syracuse, in Sicily, was built

OSSA   High mountain in eastern Thessaly, near the Aegean coast

OTHRYS   Mountain in Thessaly

PACHYNUS   Promontory at the southeastern tip of Sicily; the left hand of Typhon, pinned beneath the island, lay under it

PACTOLUS   Gold-bearing river in Lydia, near Sardis

PALICI   Pool of water in Sicily known for its natural gases

PALLAS   Another name for Minerva

PAN   A native of Arcadia, half-man, half-goat, possibly the son of Jupiter or of Apollo, and the god of forests and shepherds; the sound of his panpipes could cause panic in people

PANCHAIA   Legendary island in the Indian Ocean known for its spices

PANDION   King of Athens, and father of Procne and Philomela

PAPHOS   Son of Pygmalion and Galatea, and father of Cinyras; founder of the city of Paphos in southwest Cyprus, sacred to Venus

PARNASSUS   Mountain near Delphi, in Phocis, a country between Boeotia and Aetolia, sacred to Apollo and the Muses

PARTHENIUS   Mountain between Arcadia and Argolis

PELEUS   A king in Thessaly; son of Aeacus, grandson of Jupiter, husband of Thetis, whom he is given in marriage because he is thought the most deserving of all men, and father of Achilles

PELION   High mountain in southeast Thessaly, near the Aegean coast; the home of Chiron and other centaurs

PELOPONNESE   Great peninsula forming southern part of Greek mainland; joined to rest of mainland by Isthmus of Corinth

PELORUS   Promontory at the northeastern tip of Sicily; the right hand of Typhon, the giant pinioned by the island, lay beneath it

PENEUS   River in Thessaly and its god

PENTHEUS   King of Thebes; son of Agave, and grandson of Cadmus

PERGUSA   Lake near Enna in Sicily

PERSEPHONE   Greek name for Proserpina

PHAETHON   Son of Apollo and Clymene, and grandson of Tethys

PHAETHUSA   One of the Heliades; daughter of Apollo and Clymene, and sister of Phaethon and Lampetie

PHASIS River in Colchis, a country in Asia at the eastern end of the Black Sea

PHILOCTETES Friend of Hercules who assisted Hercules in the building of his pyre and received the bow and arrows of his friend; joined the Greeks against Troy in the tenth year of the Trojan War

PHILOMELA Daughter of Pandion, sister of Procne, and sister-in-law of Tereus

PHLEGETHON River of the underworld; its name means "burning"

PHOCAEA City in Ionia, western Asia Minor, on the Aegean coast, a center of the dye industry that obtained from mollusks a costly purple or crimson dye usually known as Tyrian purple

PHOEBUS Name for Apollo, especially as god of the sun; also refers to the sun itself

PHRYGIA Country in central and western Asia Minor

PINDUS Mountain in Thessaly

PIRENE Fountain in Corinth, sacred to the Muses

PISA City in Elis, in the northwest Peloponnese

PLEIADES Seven sisters, daughters of Atlas and Pleione, an ocean nymph

PLUTO (Greek: Hades) God of the underworld; son of Saturn and Ops, and brother of Jupiter and Neptune; also called Tartarus and Dis

PROCNE Daughter of Pandion, sister of Philomela, wife of Tereus, and mother of Itys

PROMETHEUS Demi-god; son of Iapetus, a Titan, and Clymene; a craftsman and trickster figure, he molded men out of clay and brought fire down to earth

PROPOETIDES Women from Amathus, in Cyprus, who denied the divinity of Venus; in her wrath, she made them the first prostitutes, then turned them to stone

PROSERPINA (Greek: Persephone) Daughter of Ceres and Jupiter who was abducted by Pluto; she changed Pluto's mistress, Minthe, into an herb, mint, when she discovered their affair;

Arachne's tapestry showed her seduced by Jupiter in the form of a serpent

PROTEUS   Sea-god who could change his shape at will

PSOPHIS   City in Arcadia

PYGMALION   Cyprian sculptor, father of Paphos by Galatea

PYGMIES   Dwarfs who live in Africa, India, or Scythia

RHODOPE   Mountain range in Thrace; once a woman in love with Haemus; the two were transformed into mountains for their impiety

SABAEA   Southwest Arabia; also called Sheba

SALMACIS   Water-nymph who was intent on seducing Hermaphroditus; the spring named for her in Caria, in Asia Minor, was said to make men effeminate

SARDIS   Ancient capital of Lydia, near the Pactolus River

SATURN   Son of Heaven and Earth, and father of Jupiter, Neptune, Pluto, Juno, Ceres, and Vesta; he was dethroned by his three sons, who divided his kingdom among them

SCYTHIA   Country north of the Black Sea

SEMELE   Daughter of Cadmus and Harmonia, and mother, by Jupiter, of Bacchus

SICYON   City in the Peloponnese

SILENUS   A satyr (forest god, part man, part goat) and the foster father of Bacchus

SPARTA   (Also Lacedaemon) City in the southern Peloponnese

SPERCHIUS   River in Thessaly

STYMPHALUS   Region in northeastern Arcadia, and the name of a town, mountain, and lake there; as one of his twelve labors, Hercules rid the area of foul birds

STYX   River of the underworld; the gods swore by its name to guarantee their oaths

TAGUS   Gold-bearing river in Hispania (Spain and Portugal)

TANAIS   (1) The river Don, in Scythia, often regarded as the boundary between Europe and Asia; (2) a city near the mouth of the river

TANTALUS   King of Phrygia; son of Jupiter, and father of Niobe

TAURUS   Mountain range in Asia Minor

TEREUS   King in Thrace; husband of Procne, brother-in-law of Philomela, and father of Itys

TETHYS   Sea-goddess; a Titan, daughter of Earth and Heaven; wife of Oceanus, mother of Clymene, Achelous, and Doris, among many others, and grandmother of Phaethon

THEBES   Capital of Boeotia; founded by Cadmus, who was led to the site by a sacred heifer and told by Athena to sow the teeth of a dragon, from which warriors sprang out of the ground; its walls were built by the magic of Amphion's lyre; later kings included Pentheus and Oedipus

THERMODON   River in Pontus, a country in Asia Minor on the southern shores of the Black Sea; the Amazons dwelt near it

THESSALY   District in northeastern Greece, the dwelling place of the centaurs

THETIS   A Nereid, daughter of Nereus and Doris; wife of Peleus, and mother of Achilles

THUNDERER   Epithet of Jupiter

THRACE   Country in the Balkans, northeast of Macedonia; Thracians were considered primitive and warlike by the Greeks

TIRESIAS   Theban seer who prophesied the fates of Pentheus and Narcissus; father of Manto

TIRYNS   Ancient city in Argolis, birthplace of Hercules and his mother, Alcmene; thus Tirynthian (from Tiryns) refers to Hercules or Alcmene

TITANS   Twelve divine children of Earth and Heaven; their offspring became the Olympian gods (Jupiter, Juno, etc.) and lesser gods

TMOLUS   Mountain in Lydia, in Asia Minor, and its god

TRITON   Sea-god, half-man, half-fish; a son of Neptune, he blew his horn at his father's bidding

TROY   City in northwestern Asia Minor; site of the ten-year-long Trojan War, which culminated in its destruction

TYPHOEUS   Another name for Typhon

TYPHON   Giant who challenged the Olympian gods; for his hubris he was buried beneath Sicily; sometimes said to have one hundred hands

TYRE   City on the coast of Phoenicia (Syria) known for its "purple" or crimson dye, produced from a mollusk

VENUS   (Greek: Aphrodite) Goddess of love; wife of Vulcan and mother of Cupid; she contrived to inspire gods and mortals alike with love

VULCAN   (Greek: Hephaestus) God of fire; husband of Venus; as blacksmith to the gods, he forged thunderbolts for Jupiter

XANTHUS   (Also called Scamander) River near Troy, in northwest Asia Minor

ZEPHYR   West wind

ZEUS   Greek name for Jupiter